D1499268

EMOTIONAL RESCUE

EMOTIONAL RESCUE

*How to Work with Your Emotions
to Transform Hurt and Confusion
into Energy That Empowers You*

DZOGCHEN PONLOP

A TarcherPerigee Book

tarcherperigee

An imprint of Penguin Random House LLC
375 Hudson Street
New York, New York 10014

Copyright © 2016 by Dzogchen Ponlop
Penguin supports copyright. Copyright fuels creativity, encourages
diverse voices, promotes free speech, and creates a vibrant culture.
Thank you for buying an authorized edition of this book and
for complying with copyright laws by not reproducing,
scanning, or distributing any part of it in any form
without permission. You are supporting writers
and allowing Penguin to continue to
publish books for every reader.

Tarcher and Perigee are registered trademarks,
and the colophon is a trademark of Penguin Random House LLC.

Most TarcherPerigee books are available at special quantity discounts
for bulk purchase for sales promotions, premiums, fund-raising, and
educational needs. Special books or book excerpts also can
be created to fit specific needs. For details, write:
SpecialMarkets@penguinrandomhouse.com.

ISBN 978-0-399-17664-7

Printed in the United States of America
1   3   5   7   9   10   8   6   4   2

BOOK DESIGN BY KATY RIEGEL

To Ava and Aya.

Your daily bursts of joy and loving smiles

heal all emotions on the spot.

Contents

Acknowledgments

As ALWAYS, EVERYTHING is interdependent, therefore this book is not a product of myself alone. So my appreciation goes first to all the objects of my emotions. Because of them, I have earned whatever wisdom of emotions I have. Wisdom in this book would not have shone in my confused mind without the kindness of my teachers, too many to name, but primarily my true spiritual friend Khenpo Rinpoche. Opportunities for me to share my experience of the wisdom tradition of the East were given to me by many Western organizations, in particular Nalandabodhi and the Treasury of Knowledge retreats.

This sharing, in letter and book form, is made possible by my beloved friend and patient editor Cindy Shelton, who had the consistent and excellent assistance of many of our community members, primarily Ceci Miller. I deeply appreciate everyone's support and contributions toward the materialization of this book, which I hope will be of benefit to many.

Finally, I would like to thank my agent, William Clark, for his excellent representation, and also Sara Carder, editorial director, Tarcher/Penguin Random House, for her assistance in bringing this book to publication.

Introduction

It was a beautiful fall day and I had just come out of my philosophy class. I was walking back home with my head full of theories supported by syllogisms about how "pain and pleasure duos" are created by mind and are simply mind's projections . . . blah blah blah. As I walked into my room, to my surprise, my uncle, with whom I'd had a history of difficulties, was sitting there waiting to give me the news that my father had passed away during his business trip to Bhutan. It was exactly one year since I had lost a teacher who had been the most important person in my life. All of a sudden my seemingly solid and beautiful theories and syllogisms of nonduality just vanished! No thoughts, no wisdom, just shock. Slowly but surely, a sensation of pain spread deep within my body and mind. This pain was nowhere close to my philosophical understanding of pain or, rather, the nonexistence of pain. This pain, accompanied by such vivid feelings, started me off on my lifelong exploration of my emotions.

My dad was born into a family from Litang in the Kham region of eastern Tibet, which is often likened to the "Wild West" or no man's land. People of Kham, known as *khampas*, are proud of their warrior culture, and people in Tibet usually say, "Don't mess with khampas." Even though my father grew up in the central-western part of Tibet, his parents raised him as a khampa boy. From a very young age, he showed signs of the warrior culture—always fearless and courageous, yet kind. My father ended up becoming general secretary, the highest-ranking administrator for His Holiness the Sixteenth Karmapa, revered head of his then eight-hundred-year-old spiritual institution. As a khampa person, he was a collector of swords and guns, simply for his love of the art of warriorship, and he genuinely appreciated the stories of brave warriors, which he read to me often from the time I was a little boy. Due to his sensitive and influential job as general secretary, I was aware that he'd received several credible threats against his life, and so there was some reason for him to have the necessary licenses for owning his guns. But what I saw in it all primarily was the sentimental value they held for the warrior culture of his childhood and family lineage. In the typical father-son way, we always had fun when he took me target shooting in the mountains.

Strangely enough, before my dad went on his business trip to Bhutan we were cleaning his guns. He reminded me how to take them apart and put them back together. We had a beautiful afternoon. Just before he departed, I didn't know why, but he gave me all the guns and said, "Now you are in charge. If you are a good son, you'll take good care of them." And I said, "Yes, of course." Later, there were so many questions about his death—whether it was natural or some conspiracy was involved because of his high-ranking position in an international spiritual organization. Here I was at seventeen, a devoted son left behind with so many thoughts, emotions, and guns. As they say, misfortunes don't come singly. So it happened that soon after, my mom fell ill, and she was in bed for about a year. While my siblings and I took care of her, I also had to deal with the settling of my dad's business affairs. My brother's presence and support throughout that period made everything easier. But at a certain point I realized I was at a crossroads, pulled in different directions by my wild emotions.

I thoroughly enjoyed my time in school, studying and practicing with my classmates, but at the same time I was bogged down with my many duties caring for my family. I envied my fellow students who had no extra responsibilities, nothing to do other than fully engaging in their education! The schedule and curriculum were challenging and also stimulating. Our first session started at four a.m. and classes continued until evening, with only a few breaks here and there. The teachers were the finest and very demanding. I continued my journey diligently but I had lost sight of my goal. Due to the stress of simply maintaining life, I almost dropped out of school and abandoned my spiritual pursuits. All these efforts really amounted to a single quest: to know something that would relieve the feelings of discontent that kept me up late at night studying and worrying.

Around this time, I came across a Buddhist teacher who later became the most influential person in my life and a genuine spiritual friend. His presence and instruction helped me to deal with my racing emotions and thoughts. The impact of his friendship was immediate. Under his guidance, I found a way to make the right choices. I became brave enough to follow the path of compassion and turn away from the route of a vengeful warrior. Somehow I ended up graduating first in my class, a great surprise to me to this day. In the end, I came to understand that all of this was happening in my little mind—thoughts, emotions, life, and spirituality. When I saw what a big role the emotions played in the drama of this life, I began to go deeper into this mind to find out everything I could about these energies.

I realized that whatever approach I took to deal with my emotions, I needed ways that would work with my whole life—methods that would actually make a difference. I needed to be able to see myself clearly, and to feel the emotions that touched me and colored my world every day. I recognized that when we're present in our life, we have an opportunity to discover who we are with all our confusions and suffering, and who we are *beyond* that confusion and pain. The alternative is to avoid direct contact with our experience, to hang out in a buffered world that doesn't quite soothe or inspire. As human beings, we seem to want both—we long for what's real, for adventure and meaning, but we also want to be comfortable. We want to find our spot on the beach and have a beer.

The contents of this book—*Emotional Rescue*—are rooted in my experience of the Buddhist path. The purpose of the book is to introduce certain methods for working with emotions so that gradually, step by step, we can move from being victims to partners to creative collaborators with these profound energies. While you won't find these methods in the Buddhist sutras—the discourses of the Buddha that form the body of his teachings—I think the Buddha would recognize his instructions in them. (The Buddha is very generous with his intellectual property.)

This book represents years of my own study and teaching as well as what I've learned from my students and others, people of many faiths and cultures who inhabit this modern world together. They exhibit qualities of goodness, intelligence, and compassion and yet suffer and struggle with their pain. Unfortunately, there is no one-size-fits-all solution for this pain. We are all unique, individual creatures living in remarkably varied environments. But we all have within us the power to take steps to overcome our pain and emotional suffering and in the process discover who we truly are. No matter who you are or where you're starting from, you deserve the genuine happiness that comes with that discovery.

I was born a Buddhist and in one sense have never been anything else. My family has been Buddhist for generations.

I have lived in Buddhist countries—India and Bhutan—and have been privileged to meet and learn from many of the great, historic Buddhist masters. On the other hand, I had to become a Buddhist like anyone does, by discovering the real meaning and goal of the Buddhist path. But the more we approach that real meaning and that goal, the less any label— Buddhist or otherwise—seems to stick. And the less these labels are necessary. I may call myself a lucky survivor of emotional drama, rescued by this wisdom of emotions, but the truth is I'm still finding my way on this joyful wisdom journey, with a little help from my friend.

Dzogchen Ponlop Rinpoche*
Seattle, Washington

---

* Dzogchen Ponlop Rinpoche was recognized at birth by His Holiness the Sixteenth Gyalwang Karmapa as seventh in the line of Dzogchen Ponlop incarnations and given the honorific title of "Rinpoche," or teacher and lineage holder.

PART ONE

Working with Emotions

1

Getting to Know Your Emotions

Be yourself. Everyone else is already taken.

—OSCAR WILDE

WHAT WOULD LIFE be like without our emotions? Kind of boring? Like a flat soda? Without that fizz and sparkle, we wouldn't be very interested in drinking life in. Emotions bring energy, color, and variety to our lives, but we also spend a lot of time confused by them. They can transport us to blissful peak states and drag us down to the depths of delusion and despair—and everything in between.

People are driven by their emotions to marry each other and to murder each other (sadly, sometimes the very same person they married!). Every day we get in line for this roller-coaster ride of emotion that thrills us one minute and turns us upside down the next. What are these unpredictable feelings and why do they seem to control us, rather than the other way around?

It depends on who you ask. You'll get a different answer

from a scientist, a therapist, a priest, an artist, or the usual beneficiaries of your love and loathing—your family and frenemies. There's an Asian proverb that says, "Medicine, if taken with knowledge; poison, if abused." This is how our emotions are. If we learn how to relate to our emotions skillfully, then they're like medicine, containing great wisdom; but if we lack this understanding, then they're like poison, causing great harm and suffering. While we're under the spell of our emotions, it's like we're sick. We can't wish away the aches and pains and fever. We have to let our sickness run its course or intervene with some kind of treatment.

If you understand your illness, you can take steps to heal yourself and end your suffering. But if you don't know what you're doing—if you take the wrong medicine—you could make yourself sicker. In the same way, when you understand your emotions and what makes them tick, you can work with their intense energy and start to heal your suffering.

To get real help with emotions, we have to go beyond a simple textbook understanding of them. It isn't enough just to know how many and what kinds of emotions there are. When we strip away what we think we know and look freshly at our personal experience of anger or passion or jealousy, what do we find? This is not just about recognizing what kinds of thoughts we're having. It's about discovering what our emotions are at their very core. Seeing that anger makes us want to strike back or that desire makes us want to please is just the beginning. Really getting to know our emotions is challenging, but it can be motivating, too. When we see that we're continually getting beat up by our emotions, we can become determined to learn how to rescue ourselves.

Before we reach real understanding and wisdom about our emotions, we first need a clear idea of what they are and how they work. Emotions get their power from a simple but deep-seated source: our lack of self-knowledge. For this reason, when we bring awareness to our experience of emotions, something truly amazing happens. They lose their power to make us miserable. So it's vital to see how emotions operate in our lives and how devastating their influence can be when they are in command. With this knowledge we begin to regain our independence. We begin to see how to free ourselves from those old patterns of fear, doubt, anger, pride, passion, and jealousy that have robbed us of so much happiness. We regain the power to navigate the direction of our lives.

Yet our emotions have been around so long, they're like old friends. We'd miss those familiar faces if one day they failed to show up. But we also know how they can deceive us—how they can trip us up, over and over, with their promises: *Listen to me, this time it will be different! This time, blowing up in anger is clearly within your rights! You'll feel so much better. This time, it will fill that empty place inside.*

THE THREE-STEP EMOTIONAL RESCUE PLAN

When you're feeling tormented by your emotions, what do you do? You probably look for an escape route. But you can't see your emotions the way you can see smoke or fire, so which way do you turn? You can't exactly decide, *My anger is hammering at the front door, so I'll go out the back.* If you react out of panic, without thinking it through, you might end up jumping from the frying pan into the fire. You never know what might be waiting for you in your backyard. Instead of leaving your well-being to chance, it's a good idea to have a rescue plan for those times when you find yourself on shaky emotional ground, looking for a lifeline.

The Three-Step Emotional Rescue Plan introduced in this book can help you learn the skills you need so that you can leave behind painful old habits in favor of new and more joyful ways of expressing yourself. The three steps are Mindful Gap, Clear Seeing, and Letting Go. They are progressive methods, each one building on the one before it, gradually empowering you to work with and transform even your most difficult emotions.

Briefly, Mindful Gap is the practice of creating a safe distance between you and your emotions, which then gives you the psychological space to work with their energy. Clear Seeing is the practice of looking at both the emotions and their surrounding landscape. You're trying to see a bigger picture, one that includes identifying patterns in your behavior. Letting Go is the practice of releasing stressful physical and emotional energy through physical exercise, relaxation, and, primarily, through awareness.

With each step you learn, you become increasingly familiar with the inner workings of your emotions. You begin to see through the dense outer layers that mask their true nature. Eventually, you see straight to the heart of your anger, passion, jealousy, and pride. Even ignorance and fear become transparent.

Taken together, mastering these three steps can bring about profound emotional healing. Each step can become a turning point, a place where your relationship with your emotions can change and evolve. Instead of simply struggling with your emotions, it's possible to develop a creative partnership with them. With time and practice, anxiety and doubt give way to trust and confidence. Gradually, you discover that your emotions themselves are the doorway to the freedom you're looking for—they open the way for you instead of holding you back.

In a way, this book isn't going to teach you anything totally foreign to your experience. You already have within you much of the knowledge you need to free yourself from habitual ways of reacting to your emotions. These habits are yours, after all. Who could be more familiar with them than you? It helps, however, to learn new ways of using that knowledge—your own common sense as well as insight—to see what's holding you back and what can move you forward into freedom.

What's in a Name?

Before going into the details of the Three-Step Emotional Rescue Plan (we can call it the ER Plan, for short), it's helpful to look first at the definition of "emotion." What do the dictionaries say? Once we have this basic definition, we can look at what an emotion is from the point of view of the ER Plan, which adds another dimension. If the dictionary definition said it all, it might be possible to learn just enough about our emotions to control them and minimize their pain, but we'd still have to look elsewhere for a glimpse of transcendent experience.

The basic dictionary definition, from the *Oxford English Dictionary* to FreeDictionary.com, tells us that an emotion is an intensified mental state that we experience as agitated, disturbed, or anxious, which comes with similar physical symptoms of distress—increased heartbeat, rapid breathing, possibly crying or shaking. Even the origin of the word "emotion" (from Old French and Latin) means to excite, to move, to stir up. And such feeling states are generally described as being beyond our conscious control or the power of reason.

But what about the emotions that make you feel happy? Aren't love and joy emotions, too? Yes. But states of mind like love, joy, and compassion don't ruin your day. You feel better, more clear and peaceful, because of them. So they're not regarded in quite the same way. When you're "getting emotional," you're usually not feeling so great. When the Three-Step Emotional Rescue Plan mentions "working with your emotions," it means unpacking and letting go of the heavy baggage of your pain and confusion.

THE GOOD NEWS

The Three-Step Emotional Rescue Plan views emotions from two perspectives. In an ordinary sense, of course there are "good" and "bad" emotions—those that bring happiness and those that bring despair and pain. On a deeper level, however, all emotions—whether we view them as good or bad—have a single essence that's beyond good or bad. No matter what they look like on the surface or how you judge them, emotions—at their core—are basically positive. This is good news! You're fundamentally okay, even when you're doubting yourself and struggling with messy, difficult feelings.

At heart, your emotional energies are a limitless source of creative power and intelligence that's "on" all the time—like the electrical current we put to so many uses. When you finally see straight to the heart of your emotions, this power source is what you see. Before an emotion escalates to a fever pitch or you've managed to chill it out, there's a basic energy that gives rise to it. This energy runs through all your emotions—good, bad, or neutral. It's simply an upsurge that's been stimulated by something in your environment—

like an upsurge in the voltage flowing through a power line. If it's just a slight increase, you may not notice it, but if it's a strong burst, it can give you quite a shock. That's why we have surge protectors for our sensitive equipment. It's too bad we can't wear surge protectors to modulate our temper tantrums.

It may be something internal and personal that stirs you up—a memory evoked by a familiar song. Or it could be something external, like your partner telling that same dumb joke he knows you can't stand. Think back to the last time you were really upset. Right before you got so heated up and the angry thoughts kicked in, there was a gap. Your mind's regular chatter stopped for a moment—one quiet moment without thought. That gap wasn't just empty space. It was the first flash of your emotion-to-be: the creative energy of your natural intelligence.

You might be thinking, *I like the sound of all this, but it doesn't apply to me. I'm not the creative type.* But you are creating all the time. You create your world all around you. You make choices, build relationships, and arrange the spaces you inhabit. You dream up goals, jobs, and ways to play, and generally envision the world you want. With a little help from the power of electricity, you can turn night into day. You can transform a cold apartment into a cozy home. In the same way, your emotions can brighten your world, warm you up, and wake you up with their vital, playful energy. When you feel lost, they can bring a fresh sense of direction and inspiration into your life.

CATCHING THE CRUCIAL "DUH" MOMENT

So emotions don't have to be a problem for you. Any emotion can bring a welcome sense of positive energy or the opposite—a dose of gloom and doom. It just depends on how you work with it, how you respond to the upsurge of energy. It can turn one way or the other. You might wonder then, *If the first flash of my emotion is just basic creative energy, what happens to screw it up?* Actually, quite a lot if you're not paying attention.

Imagine you're out for a walk with your partner on a nice day. You're just strolling along when suddenly you trip on a rock, and you're knocked off balance. It happens so fast that your mind goes blank for a second. But then thoughts rush in. *What the . . . ! Who left that there? I really could have hurt myself!*

At that point you have a choice. You could laugh about it, or you could get mad and look around for someone or something to blame—the Parks Department, the city council, your partner (who didn't notice and just kept walking), or the offending stone itself. Or you could stoop down to remove it from the path so the next person doesn't trip, too. You might do all of the above, in rapid succession. It's not exactly a neat, well-thought-out process.

When we see we're getting upset, we usually look outside of ourselves for the reason. We point our finger at our partner, or our neighbor, or the guy in the car who cut us off. But each time we do this, we make our habit of blaming others deeper and more troublesome. If you tend to get angry with your spouse when you don't see eye to eye, then with every disagreement it gets easier to slip into that combative pattern. You could be out for a special evening at your favorite restaurant and end up having a big blowup. But it doesn't have to be this way.

Before ruining your anniversary dinner or endangering a friendship, you can learn to recognize that moment when you've tripped mentally and are knocked off balance. There's that moment when you're startled and speechless—kind of a "duh" moment. For just a second, there's no thought, no concept to explain your experience. Yet the buzz is there, the fizz in the soda, the power surging through the lines. You're awake and alert, but you haven't yet gotten distracted by your mind's chatter about what's happening. Look at that "duh" moment, and then watch how, in the very next moment, all of the habitual reactions kick in.

When we give in to anger, each hateful, unkind thought brings on yet another jolt of angry energy, and even more negative, blaming thoughts. Almost instantly we manage to think up a story that feels true—as legitimate as the nightly news. *Something happened to me, and pardon me if I'm a little upset about it.* If we let our thoughts run on like this, our mind begins to spin. We're not sure what we're doing anymore. We lose touch with what originally happened and start reacting to our own reactions. We can't sort out or resolve an issue that's so far removed from the present moment. It's like trying to decipher a message passed from friend to friend before it's finally delivered to you by a third party. Is the meaning clear? Has anything been added or left out?

When we're upset like this and preoccupied with assigning guilt to some and acquitting others (most notably ourselves), we miss how the process works. But if we can catch this process playing out before it goes too far, we can turn our mind in a more positive direction. Then, even if we still get carried away, at least our thoughts will be more constructive and optimistic. If we don't catch any of it, we end up feeling victimized, wondering, *Why does this keep happening to me?*

You can make a commitment to being awake and engaged with your life, or you can just close your eyes and hope for the best. Like it or not, it's your choice. Either way, your emotions and thoughts will keep on coming. When no one's paying attention to them, they like to run wild. If you're slow to take notice, you might find these feelings ruling your life and stealing your precious sanity. As you come to know your emotions better, you realize they're not one-dimensional, fixed states of mind that go on for so many hours, days, or years. They come and go, rise and fade, just like our breath, which lasts only a few seconds. With a little practice, you can actually watch this happening.

Say one day you're thinking about your old girlfriend or boyfriend. You're thinking that he or she was really the right person for you and now they're gone. They moved away and took your whole comic book collection. So sad! No matter what you do, nothing cheers you up. You listen to your iPod. You watch a little TV. You're still sad. This goes on for hours. Finally you decide to get up and go for a walk. You head for the local coffee shop, and on your way, you notice vivid colors—spring flowers are popping up all over the neighborhood. You can feel the warmth of the sun on your back. Someone waves to you, and there's a nice light breeze. By the time you get to the coffee shop, you're smiling. It's a different world.

That's how it is. You think you're frozen in a painful mind state with no way out. At least that's what it feels like, no matter what logic or experience tells you. You think, *I'm never going to feel any better. I'll never be free of this hurt* (or jealousy, heartbreak, resentment, or whatever it is). But on the other side of your sadness, there's your happiness and amusement. On the other side of your anger, there's your peacefulness and gentleness. Every emotion has its flip side: when you're looking at one face, the other face is right there, too, even though you can't see it. So whichever face your emotions are showing you—whether it's happy or sad—the other side, its opposite, is always there, too.

Your sadness and joy, your anger and calm, all develop out of the same flow of creative energy. This energy can never be permanently stuck or frozen. Of course, it can get hung up, and that's painful, but something eventually gives. One minute you're so down that you can't even enjoy your favorite song, and a few hours later you're enjoying the smell of fresh coffee as you smile and wave to a friend. Your perspective returns and you think, *Oh, yeah. I'm okay. Life is good.*

DIY RESCUE NOTES

If you don't have an effective plan for dealing with your emotions, then it's hard to know how to really get free of the pain they cause. Sometimes you can stop your anger from spilling out by sheer force of willpower or through utter fear of the consequences (losing your job or your marriage). But how many times have you blown off steam one night, only to find that you're just as angry the next day? Then you have to try to cool down your anger all over again.

The key to rescuing yourself emotionally is knowledge. You resolve to learn all you can about these energies that can be as tough on you as the neighborhood bully. With a little training, you can learn how to look more clearly at emotions like anger, jealousy, or passion and see the steps you need to take to work with them and gradually transform them. Not only can you rescue yourself from their control, one day you may even come to appreciate and enjoy their pure, vital energy. And that's what this book is about.

As you prepare to work with the powerful energies of your emotions, as you get ready to free yourself from old, destructive habits, you need a strong sense of resolve to stick with it. It's a process that calls for you to work with your mind every day and to be willing to deal with discomfort now and then. At those times when you don't feel like being particularly patient or kind, this sense of resolve can support you and keep you on track. After you've had some practice, even your so-called mistakes begin to help you remember the simple, clear energy of your emotions—and just remembering instantly clicks you into that awareness.

Now you're taking a fresh look at what your emotions actually are. Consider your attitude toward those emotions. How do you feel about the feelings you're having? Do you hate them or love them? How do you treat your anger? Your sadness? Your desire? Once you figure this out, you'll have a better understanding of how to work with them. Then you can use the Three-Step Emotional Rescue Plan outlined in this book to deal with your emotions on the spot.

℘ FIRST ASK YOURSELF...
What do I want to get out of this?

Before you start to work on any long-term project that's going to require hard work at times and may be boring at other times, you'll probably want to ask yourself, *Why do I want to do this anyway?* and *How strong is my commitment to this process?* To be successful, you need to be clear about your answers. You need to have a strong resolve.

If your reasons for learning and practicing the Emotional Rescue Plan aren't clear to you, your motivation won't click in the next time you face a difficult situation. You won't stick with it, and once again you'll get beat up by your emotions. You need a real sense of purpose here. Because if you're only mindful of your emotions every now and then, how will you experience the emotional rescue you're looking for? Eventually, you'll wonder why your project isn't working, why you're not feeling any better, and whether you should give up on this method and try something else.

The purpose of the written exercise at the end of this section is to clarify your motivation. *Why would you take up mindfulness practice in the first place?* It's also meant to help you make a personal connection to the three steps that will help you achieve your goals: Mindful Gap, Clear Seeing, and Letting Go.

Before you get started, please read the guidelines for "writing mindfully." This approach to the writing will be helpful as you reflect on, and then respond to, each of the questions in the exercise that follows.

Writing Mindfully

Writing can be a key element of success in working with your emotions. Many of the exercises that follow suggest an option to do some form of written reflection. Keeping a journal (paper or digital) where you can save your writing as you go along is a good idea. Like the practice of Mindful Gap, writing mindfully can be especially helpful when we're confronted with strong emotions in ourselves or with difficult situations in our environment. When we write mindfully, we slow down our thought process. When we're focused on the physical act of writing or typing, the act of our fingers producing a flow of words, we can only write so fast. Writing mindfully can also slow the momentum of our emotional energy and give us a little more time and space to see what's going on. In this way, the act of writing can be a form of Mindful Gap practice.

Getting started

General guidelines for written exercises

- For each exercise that follows in this book, a time frame is suggested. You can write more or less, but decide how long you'll write before you start.
- As you write, pay attention to the physical sensation of your hands on the pen and paper or keyboard, and how your physical movements feel as the words appear on the page or screen.
- Pay attention to thoughts and emotions as they arise and become the written words before you.

❖ Don't stop and think; keep writing even when you don't know what to say next.

❖ If you become uncertain, write something like, "I don't know what to say." You might end up writing that several times. Or, make a note of a physical sensation you notice: Is your neck stiff? Are you thirsty or tired? Or, simply rewrite the topic or question you're addressing.

❖ After a period of writing, pause and rest your mind.

❖ Read over what you wrote at some point in time, if not right away.

❖ Suggestion: keep your writing (for at least a year) in a journal or notebook.

When you practice writing in this way, the inner critic that often chides us toward "perfection" doesn't get a chance to gain hold. As you write, simply accept whatever arises without judgment. With clear attention, let yourself write without editing.

See how this approach affects your experience of reflecting on the questions in the exercises you'll find throughout this book. You can use the same principles of mindful attention with any form of response you have to the exercises, including the ones that involve verbal and physical activities, either solo or in groups. If you choose to keep a journal, you don't have to limit it to your writing. You may also wish to use it to keep drawings or photos or other observations you make about your experiences.

What do I want to get out of this?

Contemplate the following questions briefly, and then choose one to write about for five or ten minutes:

* What is it about my emotional life that I most want to change?
* Why is this change so important—what has happened that makes it urgent?
* What do I expect from learning the techniques of Mindful Gap, Clear Seeing, and Letting Go? What would I like to see happen?
* If I could make a wish for myself that would come true—what would it be? (We are just supposing here . . . what's your real wish?)

Be as specific in your answers as you can be. General responses like, "I want to be happy," or "I wish I were a nicer person," need deeper exploration. You could start generally, and then add further details as they occur to you. Also, start with yourself and your personal goals before thinking of how you could improve the lives of others. (That will come soon enough.)

2

Mindfulness Is the Key

*Human beings can alter their lives
by altering their attitudes of mind.*

—WILLIAM JAMES

IF YOU'VE EVER sat in an airplane preparing for takeoff, you've seen the flight attendants point out the emergency exits. When the lights go down in the cabin, the exit signs remain lit. There are lights marking the aisles as well. There's a well-defined plan in place so that in the event of trouble everyone will be able to quickly and safely find their way to the nearest exit.

Likewise, when you have a clear-cut plan in place for dealing with disturbing emotions, there's no need to panic. You know what to do to find your way out of a hurtful situation. When you don't have a plan, a clear sense of direction, any fiery moment of passion can make you want to jump up and run without thinking. And that could easily lead to even more trouble.

The Three-Step Emotional Rescue Plan is designed to

help you survive emotional emergencies. It also helps you deal with the minor bruises of day-to-day living, as you bump up against others who, just like you, are trying to avoid pain and survive. As you work with the plan and test it out personally, you grow in confidence and expertise. After a while, you instinctively know what to do. You see the quickest safe way out of trouble and you just go for it. You stay relaxed and calm.

The ER Plan is easier, safer, and more effective if you're familiar with certain basic ideas right from the start. It's always a good idea to learn the fundamentals of any topic you're studying before trying to master its finer points. If you wanted to learn to fly a plane solo, for example, you'd start by learning all the parts of the airplane and how they work. Then, when you were ready to take off in your Cessna, you'd have a framework for understanding how the aircraft operates and how to get the most out of it. In the same way, when you're dealing with emotional crosswinds, it's helpful to have a good grasp of mindfulness.

Why is mindfulness important? You'll need to know what it is before you can apply Mindful Gap (the first step of the ER Plan) to the resentment you're bringing home from an awful day at work. You'll want to know how mindfulness helps, and why it's worth the effort to develop it. From the beginning, in fact, you'll need to be mindful of your general attitude toward the experience of strong emotions. Then you'll be able to extend your mindfulness, noticing how your attitude affects your reactions—your habitual ways of dealing with big emotions and painful complications.

GUARDING YOUR PEACE OF MIND

Being mindful simply means "paying attention." It's the key to working skillfully with your emotions, and to guarding your peace of mind. To be mindful also means "to remember." Even the best plan will be useless if you don't remember to do it. While mindfulness is a unique skill that can be practiced on its own, it's also a vital ingredient of all three steps in the ER Plan—Mindful Gap, Clear Seeing, and Letting Go.

So how do you go about paying attention? And what is it, exactly, that you're supposed to pay attention to? You simply bring your awareness to the present moment, to where you are right now. There's a sense of freshness and open space—a natural gap—between past and future moments. In this spot of nowness, you're aware of the thoughts and feelings that come and go, and the colors, sounds, and scents of the world around you.

You can be mindful anywhere—when you're out walking in a park or shopping at the mall, cooking dinner for your family or watching TV. You can be alone or in a crowd, happy or sad, arguing with your roommate or laughing with an old friend. You can be mindful whenever you have a thought or feeling—which is pretty much all the time.

Being mindful is not very difficult once you get used to doing it. It gradually becomes a habit that replaces the habit of mind*less*ness—forgetfulness, or spacing out. In the beginning, it's helpful if you can spend a little time by yourself getting familiar with this simple way of training your mind, also known as mindfulness practice.

℘ SHORT MINDFULNESS PRACTICE

Time: Five or ten minutes to start. Increase as desired.

Mindful Posture

To begin a session of mindfulness practice, you'll need a comfortable seat. You can sit in a chair or use a firm cushion on the floor. The main point is to have a relaxed but upright posture so that your spine and shoulders are straight. If you're sitting on a chair, place your feet evenly on the floor, and if you're sitting on a cushion, cross your legs comfortably. You can rest your hands in your lap. Your eyes can gaze slightly downward a short distance in front of you.

Mindful Breath

Once you're sitting comfortably, take a deep breath. Bring your attention to your breathing. Focus lightly on the out-breath. Then on the in-breath, simply relax. There's a sense that you're actually feeling your breath, feeling its movement. As you relax, you begin to appreciate now-ness, the present moment.

Mindful of Thoughts, Feelings, and Emotions

When thoughts come up, don't follow them, and don't try to stop them, either. Simply acknowledge their momentary presence and let them go. Return your attention to your breath. In the same way, notice any physical sensation (pain in your knee) or emotion (a flash of anxiety, moment of anger) that comes up. Acknowledge its presence, then relax, let it go, and return to your breath.

Ending Your Session

Notice how it felt to practice mindfulness for these few minutes. As you come back to your usual state of mind, remember that you can take a short break now and then to be aware of the movement of your thoughts, the movement of your breath. You can do "mini-mindfulness sessions" throughout your day, whenever you have a moment.

You'll find more extensive mindfulness meditation instructions in Part Two of this book.

Mindfulness is a way of being watchful. It's how you pay attention to whatever tries to enter the doorway of your mind. You stay mindful of the thoughts and emotions that come knocking, or leaning on your doorbell. As long as you stay alert and mindful, you get to decide whom to let in and how long they can stay. If the Terminator or Dr. Doom wanders in, you remember not to get so carried away with their story lines that you forget who's in charge. If they misbehave or overstay their welcome, you remember to ask them to leave or order them out.

Don't worry about whether you're doing this "right" or "wrong." The main thing is to give your practice your full attention. You bring yourself into the present moment by bringing your awareness to the experiences of your body, the movement of your breath, and the stream of thoughts and feelings. Whenever you notice that you've drifted away, you bring yourself back. There are two things at play here: one is your awareness of being in the present; the other is the mindfulness that sees you leaving the present and brings you back.

Mindfulness produces a quality of attention that's precise and clear. You're clear about your thoughts. You're clear about what you see, hear, and feel. When you're seeing something in a moment of nowness, you know precisely what's happening. You see your present state of mind and the habit patterns that are at work in your thinking. You're aware of what you're doing and are able to see that you have choices. You're not doomed, yet again, to spend money you don't have—you can decide you're just window-shopping for that new sports car.

Mindfulness can also help you see to what degree your habitual reactions to your emotions—the ways you deal with anger, desire, jealousy, envy, and so forth—are determined by your attitude toward them. You may not think about this kind of thing very often, but there's a lot to be learned by identifying how you look at all of those emotions and what you really think of them.

THREE ATTITUDES: NEGATIVE, POSITIVE, UNBIASED

In the scheme of the Three-Step Emotional Rescue (ER) Plan, we look at the three basic attitudes we can have toward our emotions: negative (bad), positive (good), or unbiased (beyond any good-bad labels). Based on our experience with emotions, we tend to hold one of these three attitudes toward them. We look one way at someone who slaps us across the face and insults us every time we see him, and another way at someone who pats us on the back and tells us jokes. The minute the "slapper" shows up, we tend to back off, even before we know what he's up to this time. We have a pretty good idea. When we're getting ready to meet our more relaxed and kindly friend, we're likely to look forward to it. On another level, however, it's possible to meet every type of emotion—even the more difficult ones—without prejudgment or expectation. When we can do this, there's nothing to interfere with our ability to see clearly and act wisely in the moment.

Each step of the ER Plan—Mindful Gap, Clear Seeing, and Letting Go—is linked to one of these three attitudes (negative, positive, or unbiased). Each step also provides an "exit"—a way of working with mindfulness to free yourself from chronic reactivity and its painful consequences. As you progress through the steps—first one, then two, then three—your attitude evolves, and so does your skill in working with your emotions. Over time, you reach the full development of the process—the recognition of your emotions as creative energy, beyond the polarities of "good" and "bad."

To discover your basic attitude, your starting point, try looking at what you instinctively do when an emotion pops up. Look again and again—you might be surprised. Do you shy away from anger? What's your response to expressions of affection? What do you do when someone shouts at you? Or starts to cry? Imagine that your emotions are people. Do you like to invite them over? Do you listen to them, or brush them off?

When you view emotions as **negative**, you don't see anything good in them at all. They're just plain bad company. They're painful, upsetting, crazy-making—and they exhaust you. They ruin your plans and stress you out. They can even make you physically ill. In acute cases, they're so toxic they can kill you or make you wish you were dead. (*If*

I can't have him-her-it, I might as well jump off a cliff. Sound familiar?) In fact, you see them as enemies of your happiness, like thieves who are constantly breaking in and ripping you off, stealing your sanity and your peace of mind. In this light, you see your emotions as strictly bad news, as worthless as the trash you throw out every day. This is the most common attitude of someone just starting the ER Plan, and it is linked primarily to step one, Mindful Gap.

When you view your emotions as **positive**, you do see something good in them. Although they may hurt you at times, they keep you honest with their painful lessons. Instead of only threatening your health and happiness, you can see that they're essential for your psychological or spiritual development. You're actually a better and stronger person because your emotions have challenged you and you've had to work through them. Like friends, they support you. Like medicine, they have the power to heal you. Like cast-off rubbish, they turn out to contain all kinds of interesting stuff that you can recycle and refashion into useful and beautiful things. This more optimistic attitude naturally develops after you've worked with your emotions for a while and have begun to see them in the context of larger patterns. It's primarily connected to step two of the ER Plan, Clear Seeing.

After you've fully appreciated both their negative and positive sides, there's yet a third way to view your emotions. Instead of seeing only opposition or contradiction, you see an **unbiased** wholeness. You recognize that all of your emotions spring from the same source: the spontaneous, ever-present creative energy of your own mind, your own heart. That's the natural state of the emotions we talked about—whether you're feeling anger, jealousy, passion, desire, or some combination of them all. That original, natural state is a very clear, discerning, and refined awareness. It sees the way things actually are (unlike our ordinary emotional mind, which is always revising the story).

This transcendent attitude represents the culmination of the process and is primarily connected to step three, Letting Go. When you finally arrive at this view, emotions don't blind you or mislead you. Instead of muddling your experience, your emotional energies have the opposite effect: they actually help you handle situations with equanimity, with a broader and more humane outlook.

THREE EXITS:
1. REJECT 2. RECYCLE 3. RECOGNIZE

In the event of an emotional flare-up, there are three "exits" you can head for, to free yourself from the grip of painful habitual patterns: Reject, Recycle, or Recognize. An "exit" (to return to our dictionary) is "a way or passage out," like a door or gate. It also means "to leave, quit, or go away from." In the theater, an actor "exits" the stage and leaves the action taking place there.

So when you're caught up in feelings of resentment, misery, or self-pity, how do you find your way out? The three steps of the ER Plan are the actual strategies, the game plan, for reaching these exits when you really need them. The exits reflect progressive levels of knowledge, skill, and experience. You can think of them as passageways leading from one level to another in a very realistic video game you're playing. When you've mastered one level of the game, you're suddenly able to gain entrance to a new level, where you're presented with a whole new set of challenges. Take away any one of these levels, and the game would be incomplete. In the same way, you reach the ultimate experience of your emotions as creative energy only by starting at the beginning and progressively developing your understanding and skills.

Once you're familiar with these three exits, you'll be ready to look at the specific methods of the ER Plan (in the next few chapters) that make it possible to rescue yourself when an emotional storm is brewing.

Exit #1: Reject

When you regard your emotions as negative, your first reaction is often to try to escape their uncomfortable energy by rejecting them. You want to shut them up, stamp them out, bury them. Basically, you want to seal them off any which way you can, until they can't touch you anymore.

Even as an act of pure impulse, this works as an exit temporarily. But it's not a true exit by itself, because the feelings will return. You're not really free. You haven't moved to the next level . . . yet.

In the first stage of the ER Plan, when your attitude toward emotions is that they're outright troublemakers, you use Exit #1: Reject. You mindfully stop the energy of the problematic emotion in order to keep painful feelings at a safe distance so that you don't get overwhelmed by them. At the same time, a mindful response allows space to apply an actual remedy for the pain. It begins a healing process that can open the door to the next level of the game. Step one of the ER Plan, Mindful Gap, teaches the skills to get you safely to this exit.

How do you reject strong emotions mindfully? What can you do to keep them from getting under your skin? Even if you haven't seen them in a while, treacherous emotions like anger and jealousy always seem to be close by. One night you see your girlfriend talking to her ex at a party, and all of a sudden you transform into your monster-self. You're ready to leap on this guy and bite his head off. This is when you know it would be a good idea to stop those emotions in their tracks.

But how can you stop them? You can't just stuff your annoyances, hostilities, and general craziness way down inside and then walk it all off later (or anesthetize it with beer or ice cream). Instead, you have to apply an actual remedy, something to neutralize the anger—take the sting out of it, and, eventually, help it go away. So what can you do besides just blowing off steam?

One remedy for anger is patience. Patience here means sticking with your mindfulness and continuing to watch these emotions without acting out. (More on this in Chapter 3.) Patience doesn't mean suppressing your annoyance or enduring pain without complaint. Practicing patience is like practicing preventive medicine—it prevents you from making yourself sick with rage, envy, or jealousy. But if you don't feel full of patience when you're upset, where are you going to get it?

It's like you have a headache and you want to take something for it. You go to the medicine cabinet, but it's empty. No painkillers there. So you decide to go to the drugstore for some aspirin. You make the extra effort because you know, as soon as you take two or three, your headache will go away. Likewise, when you mindfully apply patience to anger, you can be sure your anger will go away. Dr. Doom and the Terminator won't be able to take up residence in your mind.

Of course, sometimes you resist taking medicine even when you have it and know it's good for you. It's not always sugarcoated and it can be hard to swallow. The key to overcoming your resistance is knowing that the right remedy can really offer you some relief. And by committing to work with your emotions mindfully, you're not just going for momentary relief. You're beginning to take charge of your emotions instead of letting them rule over you. You're approaching a long-term cure.

When you're focused on using this exit, it's important to remember all the ways your unchecked emotional mind has wreaked havoc in your life and caused you suffering. It's the story of your past and your foreseeable future, if nothing changes. When you can see that it isn't so much the emotions themselves that are the problem, but your habitual ways of dealing with them, then you may be ready for a fresh approach. Although rejecting your emotions is often helpful, there are times when it isn't quite *enough*. No matter how diligently you try to keep an emotion in check, it keeps coming up.

When that happens, what do you do? If you just keep trying to stop it, telling yourself over and over, *I can't stand this feeling. I've got to get rid of it!* it may become even harder to break free of it. In that case, it's more useful to think, *Since I'm having this emotion right now, I'm going to look at it in a different way this time and try to make the best use of it.*

Exit #2: Recycle

When you become willing to see your emotions as positive, or potentially positive, your approach to them naturally changes. Instead of just wanting out and running for the door, you become more curious. You realize that all this emotional energy can work for you: the garbage heap is worth a second look. In step two of the ER Plan—Clear Seeing—your passageway to relief is Exit #2: Recycle. At this point, you no longer want to entirely stop the energy you've been rejecting and throwing out. Instead, you want to reclaim and recycle it—redirect it toward some positive purpose.

These days all kinds of useful things are made out of so-called garbage. The very same stuff that somebody tosses out as junk today could become a new pair of shoes, a cool backpack, or a sculptural coffee table tomorrow. And when you have a habit of recycling, you produce less waste overall. Generating less garbage and more renewables benefits you personally and helps your community, too.

In the same way, any emotion can be seen as negative or positive, as worthless or full of potential. It just depends on how you look at it and how you handle the energy. Your sadness, discontent, and vanity can be both the contents of your garbage bin *and* the useful stuff you make by recycling it.

How do your emotions transform from garbage into a nice pair of shoes? How does an emotion go from something so repulsive you don't want to look at it to something not only attractive but comforting and central to your happiness? You don't toss out these feelings unexamined—you pay attention to them and look closely at their qualities. When you get to know your emotions, they don't seem so frightening. You begin to appreciate how they can be just the friend, the helper, and the medicine you need.

Step by step, you begin to see past your biases to the positive side of your emotions. You glimpse their transformative potential. You see how the very sharpness of your anger has a quality of clarity and precision. You start to get a more refined understanding of how the emotions work—

suddenly you know how to resolve that conflict at the office. That same energy can help you cut through hesitation and take a step in a new direction. If you're feeling sad, rejected, and hopeless—you've lost a job or a love—the energy of those emotions, too, can become a source of insight and inspiration that you can apply to all kinds of things. You begin to see that there is no emotion you have to throw out. You can recycle them all. Just as the venom of a poisonous snake can be transformed into lifesaving medicine, even toxic envy can be transformed into life-affirming kindness.

Say an old friend writes a song that goes viral one day, and then almost overnight she makes an album and starts her own record label. You see her beaming face every day on your iPad or smartphone and you begin to feel jealous. Instead of crying because you're still working at Java Joe's, what are you going to do? You can catch the emotion that's arising and reprocess it, first by acknowledging your envy and remembering to mindfully watch the doorway of your mind. When you see who's knocking, trying to make an entrance and grab your attention, you can invite them in, but set some ground rules. No bad behavior or running around. They can stay for a while for some honest conversation. Why did they come? What's worrying them? As they find a way to say what they want to say, gradually the rhetoric softens. There's room for sympathy. Your envy starts to transform into appreciation and happiness for your friend's good fortune. Then, instead of dragging you down, it may even inspire you to realize your own dream.

The ER Plan helps you develop the knowledge and skills to redirect your energy by taking Exit #2: Recycle. Over time, you start to view your emotions as basically good—like friends, supportive of your happiness and growth. With this more positive attitude, your approach is to engage your emotions, to go ahead and feel them, while at the same time exploring their potential. Given a chance and a little understanding, what might they become?

At this point, you're discovering that your emotions can be more productive than destructive. You don't have to get discouraged when a strong feeling comes up and you start to spin out or lose your grip. That very emotion has within it the resources you need to break the pattern. Its intensity can potentially wake you up, shake you loose from your preconceptions. Your emotions are the sparks, the fizz, that inspire you to transform your struggles and frustrations into beautiful music and poetry. Sure, they're the source of your heartbreaks, but they're also the source of your healing and compassion.

Exit #3: Recognize

When you arrive at the point of regarding your emotions as creative energy, your approach to them naturally changes again. You gain access to the next level by aiming for Exit #3: Recognize, where you bypass the efforts of rejecting or recycling. Instead, you go straight to the heart of the emotion and connect with its vivid energy just as it is—so vibrant that it penetrates all those layers of fixed ideas and habits that mask its true nature. Letting Go, step three of the ER Plan, is the method that leads you to this exit.

When you can accept your emotions just as they are, you're able to see them freshly, with new eyes. You begin to recognize the intelligence and compassion that are always there, at the heart of your emotions. You see in them the clear, wakeful qualities of wisdom, rather than the old familiar faces of confusion.

At this point in the game, you've noticed that the "either-or" point of view (good versus bad) doesn't make sense for all of your experiences. There are emotions that hold many different feelings at once and still seem to resonate a single, if inexpressible, message. It's hard to say anything about them without reducing their impact.

Such instances aren't that exceptional. One day you're feeling bored and dissatisfied with your life. You're flipping through a travel brochure, wishing you were a thousand miles away sitting on a picturesque shore at sunset. You're getting unhappier by the moment. Then for some reason you glance up and notice the beauty of the sunset right in front of you. Your mind stops and you simply take it in. The picture you see is larger than any label you can place on it. It takes you beyond words.

Such moments can be transformative if you notice them. They can shift your way of seeing. It's like you've set aside all your brochures and scripts and are simply living in a vivid present. There's a flash of wholeness—you're not separate or alienated from your surroundings.

As long as you're still working with your emotions by rejecting or recycling them, you're taking a less direct exit from pain and struggle. You have to either get rid of your emotions or else transform them before you can free yourself from their suffering. Even when you've begun to appreciate your fear and anger as recyclable and potentially beneficial, a slight sense of dissatisfaction remains: you think something still is not quite right with these feelings. Though you see the value of them, you think they aren't good enough just as they are—you feel you *must* transform these emotions into something better.

When you're headed for Exit #3, however, there's no need to change your emotions into something different. At this point, you can take your emotions in their pure state. You embrace them just as they are. You don't try to get rid of them, thinking they're nothing but garbage, and you also don't try to change them, thinking they have great potential to become eco-shoes or a rubber purse. You go beyond both these views when you recognize the tremendous clarity, insight, and compassion that are the real nature of emotions. When you can connect with their essence, their original state, emotions are simply vibrating energy—the creative play of your natural, inborn intelligence.

Once you see the network of connections that links you and your emotions to your pain and suffering or to your freedom and happiness, you can go beyond theory and start planning exactly how to deal with your strong feelings when they're happening in real time.

ᕂ ASK YOURSELF . . .

How do I remember
what I'm doing and why I'm doing it?

Even when your intention to work with your emotions is clear, and you're determined to carry through, you can forget to do it. You get busy and other things grab your attention. *Mindful Gap, what's that again?* Your old patterns start to creep back in, and soon you're suffering from the same old complaints, all your familiar aches and pains. It's like getting good medicine from the family doctor, but then forgetting to take it. If you do that, you shouldn't be too surprised when you don't get well.

This exercise can help you remember your intention, your motivation, for working with your emotions. It puts this Emotional Rescue project on your calendar.

Take Action

Identify some specific actions you will take. For example:

 ❖ I will _____ (e.g., set aside half an hour to contemplate twice this week: at seven a.m. on Tuesday and Saturday).
 ❖ When I _____ (e.g., wake up in the morning), I will _____ (e.g., review my intention before I get involved in other things).

❖ When I _____ (e.g., go to bed at night), I
will _____ (e.g., reflect on my intention and
review whether I was able to carry it into my
actions during the day).

Try this for a while. Then think up a different scheme.
Use activities connected to your home, workplace, or
even leisure time to help you "remember"—be creative!

THE THREE-STEP EMOTIONAL RESCUE PLAN

Connecting the 3 Steps with the 3 Phases of the process

PHASE 1 *"just beginning, getting the hang of it"*

❖ Primary view of your emotions . . .	Negative: fearful/toxic/ overwhelming/unwholesome/ garbage/dangerous
❖ Primary step applied . . .	Mindful Gap: feel, hold, look
❖ Primary exit accessed . . .	Exit #1 Reject: stop the energy or leave the situation

PHASE 2 *"more familiar, changing the game"*

❖ Primary view of your emotions . . .	Positive: challenging but workable/wholesome/useful for personal development
❖ Primary step applied . . .	Clear Seeing: getting the big picture (based on experience with Mindful Gap)
❖ Primary exit accessed . . .	Exit #2 Recycle: reprocess the energy Exit #1 available as needed.

PHASE 3 *"effortless dance, everything flows together"*	
❖ Primary view of your emotions . . .	Creative Energy: beyond "good–bad," inexpressible clarity, compassion, wholeness
❖ Primary step applied . . .	Letting Go: releasing bound up, stressful emotional energy through body–mind relaxation (based on experience with Mindful Gap and Clear Seeing)
❖ Primary exit accessed . . .	Exit #3 Recognize: seeing the awakening, enriching qualities of an emotion's energy, just as it is Exits #1 and #2 available as needed.

3

Help Is on the Way

*The road to success is always
under construction.*

—LILY TOMLIN

As LONG AS we're just discussing theory, working with our emotions sounds easy. But as soon as it gets real—your boss hands you a pink slip, your daughter skips school, or your partner doesn't like your new haircut—then suddenly it's a different story. What seemed so simple when you first read about it—being mindful and stopping yourself before you say something regrettable—isn't always so easy in a heated moment. You think, *I really have to say this one thing right now, just to make my point, and that'll be it. Then I'll stay cool.* But it's never just one thing, is it? You give your habitual tendencies just one little inch, and before you know it they've taken you miles down the road on that same old trip you swore you never wanted to take again. Same scenery, same suffering.

If this sounds familiar, don't give yourself a hard time about it. That hasn't helped in the past, and won't help you now, either. What will help is to have a plan. In the event of sudden strong emotion, you won't have time to stop and map one out.

THE THREE-STEP EMOTIONAL RESCUE PLAN: ALTERNATIVES TO BEING YOUR OWN WORST ENEMY

The Emotional Rescue Plan consists of three simple steps, Mindful Gap, Clear Seeing, and Letting Go. Whenever you're feeling disturbed or overwhelmed by your emotions, you can use these methods to immediately calm yourself and relieve stress from your situation. As a result of practicing these three steps, you'll gradually begin to see how you get caught up over and over in patterns of behavior that hurt you instead of help you.

Of course your intention is always to get out of trouble instead of into it, to relieve emotional pain instead of intensify it. But often what you do has the opposite of the desired effect. You're your own worst enemy when it comes to choosing between a knee-jerk reaction and a cool, tempered response to a friend's insensitive remark about your choice of romantic partner. Or to your boss's praise of the new hire's ideas (so like the ones you just mentioned to her before the meeting). Or it may be just a feeling of irritation that simmers in the background begging you to snap at the kids or the dog or the clerk at the grocery store.

Your habitual patterns—your automatic reactions to the energy of your emotions—prompt you or even push you to do what you do over and over again. No matter that ten seconds later you're feeling embarrassed, foolish, or just plain stupid. What you'll learn in this book, as you go through the steps of the Emotional Rescue Plan, will help you free yourself from these persistent and persuasive patterns. We know from recent research in neuroscience that simply practicing step one, Mindful Gap, for a few minutes can have a significant impact on your ability to make fewer errors, make better decisions, and let go of poor choices.

In the beginning, you concentrate solely on step one. When that becomes familiar and natural to do, add step two. Finally, go to step three and explore that. You'll reach a stage where your emotions and the instructions for working with them come to you almost simultaneously. It gives you the kind of confidence you get from having a good education and a little money in your pocket.

As you read on, be aware that what's being presented here is a detailed look at this three-step method, so it may seem like a long, drawn-out deal. But in actual practice, each step of the process moves quite a bit faster. Now let's consider step one, Mindful Gap.

Mindful Gap

In the UK there's an underground transit system, nicknamed the Tube, that serves London and neighboring areas. When the train pulls up and its doors open, a recorded voice comes over the sound system saying, "Mind the gap." It's a reminder to passengers to watch for the open space between the station platform and the train as they board, to prevent accidents. "Mind the gap" is such a part of the London experience that the slogan was made into a T-shirt for tourists.

If you're stepping onto the Tube in London, you have to mind the gap because you don't want to fall in and get injured. When you're working with your emotions, though, you "mind the gap" a little differently. In the moment when you're having strong feelings, it's every bit as dangerous not to be mindful of the gap between yourself and your emotions.

Mindful Gap has three parts: Feel, Hold, and Look. It starts with remembering to be mindful—not forgetting to look and see who's knocking at the doorway of your mind. If you're fortunate enough to catch the first moment a disturbing emotion strikes, that's great. But it's also good if you can catch the offending party after all the commotion has begun. That's better than not noticing anything until it's all over and peace and quiet have returned.

Here's how step one of the ER Plan—Mindful Gap—works. We'll use anger as an example because we all feel it and it's always difficult.

When Emotion Strikes . . .

❧ STEP ONE:
Mindful Gap means to . . .

❖ Feel—stop and just FEEL the energy. Don't block it and don't react to it.

❖ Hold—don't replay what just happened and don't fast-forward to a future moment.

❖ Look—at your emotion "face-to-face" to see its natural state—a sense of curiosity helps!

MINDFUL GAP: FEEL

The FEEL part of Mindful Gap is our starting place. What does it mean to "feel"? Something happens—an email informing you that your rent is going way up—and you notice you're getting angry. The instant you recognize that, you stop everything and just FEEL it. Don't block the energy, but don't react to it, either. That's it. You don't need to do anything at this point. Just stay mindful and aware of what you're feeling.

When you take time to feel your anger, everything naturally slows down. You turn your attention inward. Right away you notice there's space to breathe, so you're not overwhelmed. In this space, you discover a gap between yourself and the anger you're feeling. That little bit of distance shows you that you're separate from your emotions. You're not just that mad agitation. You're also the one who's observing it. If you and your anger were exactly the same, how could you be watching it?

That's the essence of Mindful Gap. It's like a safe driving habit. In driving school, the student drivers learn to keep a certain amount of distance between their car and the car in front of them. If you're following this rule and the car ahead of you stops or turns suddenly, you have time to step on the brake and avoid a collision. If you're driving too close, you're more likely to have a painful, costly accident.

This is different from pushing away your anger impulsively with the intention of cutting all ties to it. Here, you're staying in touch with the energy. You're willing to feel whatever comes up, from life's petty annoyances to the trials of loss, fear, and grief. Say you're on a nice trip with your partner, and she complains about the hotel and criticizes your driving. If you can think to yourself, *Mindful gap, mindful gap* . . . just as your irritation starts heating up, you can avoid a messy confrontation and instead find a way to communicate.

It's important to remember that any story you're telling yourself (*He doesn't understand*; *I keep trying, but . . .*) and the feeling it's based on (hurt, annoyed) are not necessarily the same. When you say, "I feel like you're always criticizing me," to your partner, you're still looking outward. It's not really a description of what you're feeling—it's more about what your partner is doing. A statement like that is part of the story line and probably closer to describing your thoughts than your feelings. On the other hand, if you say, "I feel so angry," that's looking inward and getting closer to the basic energy of your emotion. At that point, try to shift your attention to your body. What sensations do you notice? Is there throbbing in your head? Tension in your jaw or shoulders? Do you feel faint or fluttery? Bringing mindfulness to physical feeling helps you let go of obsessive thinking about what got you upset. Relax as much as you can. When worry and fault-finding thoughts come up, let them go and simply refocus on how you feel in your body and mind. This takes courage. You have to be willing to FEEL, even when you want to shut down.

You can find all kinds of ways to avoid feeling. If you catch yourself thinking, *I don't want this! I don't need this*, and then running for a drink or to Facebook, you may be just looking for a distraction. Your social conditioning may say, *This isn't the right time or place*, or *You should be strong*. But your emotions are trying to tell you something, too. What's going to happen if you refuse to stop and listen? It will lead to more grief. If you lock your feelings away in the basement, hoping for peace and quiet, they'll just start making an annoying racket, like a whining puppy.

At this point, you may be thinking, *What kind of a plan is this, if I have to feel terrible? How is that going to help?* Don't worry, the decision to FEEL is just the beginning of working with this anger. Your mindfulness has created an opening, a gap, that wasn't there before. This allows you to see a way forward, but you're still not in the clear.

MINDFUL GAP: HOLD

The HOLD part of Mindful Gap is where you actually dig in and get a good look at what's been bouncing you around. You've already changed the game by slowing everything down and feeling your anger. Now at HOLD, you push the "pause" button, which keeps you in the present moment. You continue to feel the energy of your anger. You stay with the experience, watch it mindfully, but you don't react to it. You don't rewind and replay what was just said or done. You also don't fast-forward to a future moment where you'll say all the brilliant things you meant to say the first time. You just hold still in the living, breathing present.

At this point, there's nothing much to do except relax and pay attention. If you're doing something, then you're probably not holding still. You're probably not sitting back and relaxing, where you can really see what's going on. Sometimes doing nothing is all you can do. If you're feeling anger, you can't really avoid it. It's like being stuck in traffic. No matter how much you wish you had taken the other road or how late it's going to make you, you can't do anything about it. So, what are your choices? You can struggle and make yourself miserable, or you can relax. Likewise, when you first start practicing HOLDING, you may feel like you're stuck in traffic. Your emotional speed is suddenly cut, but you have a hard time gearing down. You could be enjoying a peaceful moment if you weren't vibrating in your seat, itching to step on the gas again.

If you're genuinely HOLDING, just "being there and relaxing," how does that help you? If you can stick with the intensity of an emotion for a little while—even for ten minutes—it's a powerful and eye-opening experience. At first you may need to be alone to do this. You might want to go someplace where you can close the door and no one will disturb you. As you get better at it, you'll be able to do it whether you're alone at home or in the middle of a heated debate on a city street. If you can observe your anger without getting lost in irate thoughts that just create a more elaborate story line, you'll see how your feeling begins to change and evolve naturally, all on its own, without any input from you. If you don't stick with it, however, you won't see what happens. You'll miss seeing all of the subtle movements that your anger undergoes. When you just HOLD still, you can watch the energy shift and change. You'll see it grow stronger, then weaker. It gets interrupted by other emotions. It changes its story. It stops being anger and suddenly turns into jealousy or passion. Your emotional experience isn't just one solid continuous thing. It's a constantly changing process.

In the same way that FEELING takes courage, HOLDING takes patience. Patience doesn't mean simply being passive, just gritting your teeth through the pain and waiting it out. The essence of patience is staying with whatever you're feeling without reacting to it, again and again, in the moment, each time it returns. And as you continue to HOLD that feeling and stay with it, try to do so with an open heart. Try to experience your emotions without any preconceived notions, without thinking of them as bad or useless right off the bat. The whole process is about relating with your emotions in a friendly and skillful way. You're not trying to stop them from coming up—you're letting them come up in whatever way they naturally do, and just watching the show.

If you can simply sit with an intention to be mindful of your experience, to FEEL and HOLD as the emotion emerges and runs its course, you'll have a chance to see not only how the emotion itself changes, but also how your perception of it changes. You'll notice how your labels for it—what and who you thought the emotion was all about—begin to change, too. Maybe you thought that job you applied for was your dream job, and when you didn't get it you were beside yourself with grief. But as you watch your feelings of distress, you also see a touch of relief in there, too, because now you don't have to move to another city. Or you see how attached you were to making your parents proud by landing this job. On the other hand, if you really wanted this job—or seriously needed it—then sticking with your feelings and witnessing all they have to reveal can help you let go of your regrets and see how to move on. Whatever unfolds, you'll look differently at your original desire for the job and why it was so important. Seeing that there's more than one way to look at the situation can help you discover your true desires and where you want to go. As you watch this process over time, you'll gradually be able to experience your emotions with a sense of real openness and mental freedom.

Sometimes we get frustrated and think, *Well, I've tried everything, but the same emotion keeps coming up again and again. This is torture!* That may seem like a fair statement, but actually that's not what's happening. Each time you experience an emotion, it's fresh—it's a whole new moment of anger or jealousy or passion or pride. It's not the same old rage and embarrassment you experienced yesterday, and the day before, and that time when you were sixteen and your dad wouldn't let you have the car. No, it's a brand-new emotion in this brand-new moment.

Although your experience "now" could remind you of your experience "then"—sometime in the past when you felt hurt or humiliated in a similar way—that moment is over. Those old feelings cannot follow you around your whole life. You are different now. Your circumstance and surroundings are different. Whatever you're feeling in this moment is unique and unrepeatable. That doesn't mean there is no connection or no value in contemplating your past experiences. That can yield important insights. But seeing the difference between "the same" and "similar" can be liberating. The sunrise this morning is beautiful, but not in exactly the same way as the sunrise yesterday or tomorrow. That realization of newness and freshness—and connection—can inspire you to stay curious, to see what you can discover about this moment while it's here.

Mindful Gap: LOOK

The last part of Mindful Gap is where you LOOK. Your looking can be different now because your experiences practicing FEELING and HOLDING have already taught you a lot. You have a deeper understanding and a much clearer view of your emotions. You're almost an expert at dealing with them compared to the newbie you were when you started to FEEL. So what more is there to know?

At this point, you've had enough of being duped by your old patterns, so with a strong sense of resolve, you look face-to-face at whatever form of intensity is knocking at the door of your mind. You look at your anger, passion, envy, or sadness without any filters. The purpose of a camera filter, for example, is to alter the amount of light to improve what an image looks like or to add special effects. Here, you're not trying to improve the looks of Dr. Doom or the Weird Sisters. You're not trying to give your feelings a makeover so they'll be nicer-looking, more polite, or more terrifying. You're not fitting them into cultural stereotypes or dressing them up Hollywood-style. You're not adding any ideas of your own. When you "look nakedly" at your emotions, you're seeing them in the raw—au naturel. They aren't wearing any conceptual or philosophical clothing.

How is this "looking" different from what you've been doing all along? You've already seen that your emotions are more fluid than you thought. The difference is that now, when you LOOK nakedly at the experience of emotions, you begin to see even further. At this point, you can see your emotions as both momentary and full of space—they're like flashes of light or the bubbles in your drink. There's a spark of anger, and then another spark. They rise and subside, flicker and pop, alive only in the present moment, in the space of nowness. These sparks are related, but they aren't the same and they don't last. They're new in every moment. What you realize now is that it's the very nature of emotions to be constantly moving and morphing. It's how emotions are. It's what they do. This is a very profound insight, and it changes your relationship to your emotions forever.

Emotions have been misunderstood for so long. Most people look at them the same way they look at all the objects and possessions in their lives, from mountains to coffee cups—as solid, continuous, and long-lasting things. Do you ever question that? Have you ever put one of your emotions on the spot by asking it, *Are you really what you seem?*

Most of the time we take our first impressions for granted and accept them as reality. We see a guy on the street and it takes us a matter of seconds to label him as "safe" or as a shady character who might rob or kill us. But what are our criteria? Hairstyle? Clothes? Unless we're very intuitive types, we're just reacting to a fashion statement or some vague feeling about social class. That's not much different from the way most of us get mad and react all the time. We don't take time to look and really *see*. If we did, it would make a big difference. A woman bumps your arm in the grocery store aisle. You're instantly irritated and condemn her as thoughtless, stupid, and clumsy until you see the tired look on her face and the three little kids hanging on her arms. As soon as you see the reality, the whole situation, your annoyance quickly disappears and you're full of sympathy.

When you're able to see that momentary nature of your feelings, all your efforts at mindfulness are starting to pay off. At last you're experiencing the true nature, the natural state, of all emotions—how they actually are. You see how it is that anger comes and goes in a quick succession of moments. You realize that it's not continuous like a rope or a chain. In fact, you have to keep it going. Unless you keep thinking these angry, blaming, get-even thoughts, the anger just fades away. When you don't feed this angry energy, it naturally dissolves and re-arises as a little less angry. You can start to experiment with it. Try feeding your anger a positive thought—a kind, compassionate, forgiving thought—and then see what happens.

In this third part of Mindful Gap, your LOOKING does two things. It shows you the way forward in working with your emotions, and it transforms your perception in a fundamental way. Once you've gotten over the idea of emotions as "things" that are unchanging and continuous, you see how flexible they really are. You can relate to anger as a supple, mobile energy instead of something tough and solid, and this leads to a feeling of release. The main thing to remember is this: your emotions, in their natural state, are nothing but pure, creative energy. You can learn to use and direct this energy in a skillful way.

Now you can see the play of emotions with new eyes, appreciating the beauty of their fluid movements. It's like watching a great yoga instructor perform a series of intricate postures in a continuous flow—so graceful and effortless, like a cloud dancing in air. When you look at your emotions in this way, you don't need to force yourself to change your attitude toward them. Instead of trying to escape from a bully, you're admiring a dance. Your focus just naturally shifts to a more positive and friendly view. From this vantage point, you can see clearly.

The more you practice these techniques, the more skilled you'll become at observing and transforming your emotional states by giving yourself a little space from them. When you mind the gap (FEEL, HOLD, and LOOK), you can stop your emotions from disturbing your mind and keeping you locked in painful behavior patterns. So when emotions come up, mind the gap. First *feel* them, then *hold* still without reacting, and then *look*—look at the gap. Feel it, experience it, and then see what happens.

ༀ ASK YOURSELF . . .

What am I feeling right now?

What's your emotional temperature right now, in the present moment? You can always stop a minute and take a reading, while you're getting ready for work, paying bills, or watching TV. Sometimes you don't notice signs of distress because they're mild and you're used to them. Other times you may feel you're about to lose your head. You can use these simple questions to pause, check in with yourself, and shift gears.

- ❖ What emotion am I feeling now? Am I *angry*, or *afraid*, or *sad*? Or spaced out?
- ❖ How intense is the feeling on a scale of 1 to 10 (if 1 is mildest and 10 is strongest)?
- ❖ What's the texture of the feeling (i.e., sharp, dull, knifelike, vibrating, etc.)
- ❖ Does the feeling simply fade or does it turn into another emotion?

Notice that you'll get different answers at different times, because conditions can differ, and our emotions are so expressive.

4

Getting
the Big Picture

*It's not what you look at that
matters, it's what you see.*

—HENRY DAVID THOREAU

STEP TWO IN the ER Plan, Clear Seeing, is the natural result
of practicing Mindful Gap, again and again, in moments of
strong emotion. If you can "mind the gap" (Feel, Hold,
Look) when you're so upset you feel like jumping out of
your skin, right away you've given yourself more breathing
room. There's a sense of greater space, and in that greater
space you see a more complete picture.

You don't want to ignore the big picture in an emotionally charged situation. That's like cruising through a busy
intersection without looking left or right. Of course, you
could sail through untouched if you're lucky. But if you're
not, you might crash into another car or hit a pedestrian.
Likewise, when you're heading toward an emotional crossroads or a critical moment in a relationship, you need to be
paying attention if you want to avoid a disaster. You could

be certain you have a clear view of the road ahead, only to discover that you missed a few warning signs: CAUTION— SLIPPERY CONDITIONS, REDUCE SPEED AHEAD.

When that happens, you could find yourself skidding out of control—trying to steer clear of a painful accident. What's in the big picture here? There's the road, the weather conditions, your sense of being in a hurry, and maybe the argument you just had on your cell phone, not to mention the police car on the side of the road. Taken together, all of these elements have an impact on whether you arrive home safely, without a big dent in your car or your pocketbook.

WHAT'S IN THE BIG PICTURE?

Clear Seeing means you're not just registering individual things anymore—a moment of anger, the broken vase—you see the setting. It's clear to you where the anger is taking place and who and what else is nearby. It's similar to a long shot or wide shot in a photograph that shows people and objects in relation to each other and their surroundings. Say, for example, you see a beautiful flower. Is it growing wild, in a garden, or for sale for $9.99 at Garden Palace? Does the setting affect how you view the flower? Does seeing the flower affect how you look at the setting?

Or say you feel a sudden onset of insecurity and self-doubt. What's in the big picture? When you become aware of the different elements in your environment, you begin to see relationships. Seeing how you feel inside, on the one hand, what's going on outside, on the other, and what it feels like when those two meet—that's seeing a more complete and brilliant picture.

Say you go for a walk in the neighborhood, still feeling worried and insecure. You see someone who lives nearby. You haven't actually met, so you're not sure whether to say hello or keep your head down. There's a moment it could go either way—for both of you. If you look up and see a friendly smile, you may feel a surge of happiness and confidence. The day seems brighter, and you say hello without hesitation to the next neighbor you meet. Friendliness and trust expand just a little on your block in those moments—and may keep growing and touching people's lives for years. The big picture is never about just one thing—a single moment or person. It's seeing the togetherness of you and your world and how nothing happens in one place (or one mind or heart) without impacting someone or something else at the same time.

The more clearly you see the relationship of your outer and inner worlds, the more likely you are to see patterns in those relationships. And when you look mindfully at those patterns, you begin to see the causes, or triggers, that can initiate a chain reaction of negative—or positive—events. When you see things this precisely, you're not so easily fooled. You can respond more skillfully to what's happening. You're not necessarily led astray by the jealous, proud, or stupid voices of the emotions buzzing in your head. You might even be more likely to listen to the voices of others and not cling so stubbornly to your own ideas.

FINDING YOUR FOCUS

In step two of the ER Plan, Clear Seeing, you're trying to see the emotion—the fear or anger—that's in front of you right now. You want to see it without distortion, and you want to see what triggers it. You also want to notice where it typically shows up for you—at the dinner table with family, at work with a particular person, or alone when there are no distractions.

You may think you know your emotions well (even too well), but when you step back and look again, these feelings can look quite different. Usually we stick too close to our emotions, and as a result, we become completely identified with them and everything we think about them. We can lose all sense of proportion and good judgment. It's like leaving a long, sensitive conversation with a friend with just a single angry word banging around in your head. Everything else is lost—a whole spectrum of rich feeling. That's the opposite of Clear Seeing.

It's easy to be fooled when we're so close to something that there's no contrast or reference point. Of course, it can be interesting and even instructive to zero in on that level of detail—like seeing the dots in those super-magnified comic strips from sixties pop art—but we don't want to get caught there. To see what's really going on, we have to pull back and look at the whole image from a distance.

As the picture comes into sharper focus, we see not only our suffering and hopes and fears, but also what others might be feeling and needing in that moment. And eventually we see even further—how past situations unfolded in a similar way and led to the same painful point.

CREATING YOUR EMOTIONAL PROFILE

As you practice Clear Seeing, you gradually develop a picture of who you are emotionally. To get to this point, first you need to reflect on your emotional patterns. Which ones keep coming around and bothering you day after day? Next, consider which emotions are strongest and most difficult to work with, and try to identify what makes them such a challenge for you.

When you know which emotions are most intense and problematic, especially if there are certain ones that cause you to fall into some kind of destructive behavior—such as hitting or pounding (physical), shouting or yelling (verbal), or thinking about hurting yourself or others (mental)—you're forewarned. If none of your emotions give you that level of trouble, that's good news. But if one of them does, then seeing and acknowledging that is the first step to dealing positively with it—or with them; like so many people, you may be struggling with two or three kinds of difficult feelings at any given time.

Taking time for personal reflection is important. Settling for an all-purpose explanation—just thinking about what emotions are and how they work for everybody—isn't enough. At this point, generalizations are meaningless. Whatever your experience, it's unique to you. Real positive change happens by diving into your own experience, and to do that you have to let go of the ideas and words that keep you floating on the surface. If you're writing a research paper on emotions, then a broad-spectrum theory is fine—and it may get you a passing grade. But if you're trying to free yourself from the suffering emotions cause you, then just knowing a basic theory won't help. You need to relate to your emotions personally.

Developing a relationship with your emotions is a lot like developing a relationship with another person. It takes some honest work. Whether you're dealing with an old friend or discovering possibilities with someone new, first you need to be able to see the other person clearly. What are their qualities and habit patterns? How does the connection between you work? Before you can resolve anything, you have to get to know that individual and look at the relationship as it is.

It can be a little more complicated with our emotions, because it's not just one relationship to one feeling that we're sorting out. We have so many feelings and shades of feelings that we can't always tell them apart. *Am I angry, or irritated, or sad today? Or am I really just jealous that Amy is getting her way again?*

As you continue to explore your feelings, eventually you'll get to know all of them quite well. Then you'll be able to see what each emotion is like for you personally—how it tends to come up, where you feel it in your body, where it goes when you chase after it with your thoughts, and so on. Without this kind of knowledge, it's impossible to free yourself from repeating the painful things you think, say, and do—criticizing yourself or others, or shutting out those who care about you—when you get upset.

When you practice Clear Seeing with a specific emotion, try not to speculate or take anything for granted. All you need to do is observe the situation. Try to see as many factors as you can that went into creating it. Then you reflect on it. This doesn't mean you ask, *Why?* and start thinking up explanations or justifications. Instead, it's like being curious. You want to know. You're doing a fact-check: *What happened here? How did such a strong wave of anger come up? I was just standing there, playing with my phone, when my girlfriend gave me this "look." I know that look—she's unhappy about something! Then I started thinking, "What did I do now? Here we go again."*

You don't need to rush to any conclusion. Give yourself time to settle down and take in the bigger picture. The whole thing could be over in a flash. But if each offended party starts thinking up further insults and abuses, it can go on and on with round after round of hurt feelings and general craziness.

EMOTIONS THAT LIKE TO HIDE

If you're constantly irritable, critical, or spaced out, you're probably well aware of the fact. It's right out there for everyone to see, including you. What's more easily missed are the subtle, suppressed, and hidden emotions that operate beneath the surface of your everyday awareness. Sometimes they're even more dangerous than the ones that get all your attention. They can be like the powerful rip currents flowing beneath the ocean's surface that can sweep unsuspecting swimmers out to sea.

When there's nothing dramatic happening, you may feel free from the tug of emotion. You're not being carried away. You're not shouting at anyone or falling apart. You're feeling pretty good, in fact. But there could still be an undercurrent of emotion affecting your life indirectly. You don't know why, but somehow you don't feel completely open and relaxed. Something in the background is nagging at you. As hazy as it is, that hidden emotion may be controlling how you see, feel, and think, just a little or a lot, depending on your personal history and emotional patterns.

Besides the hidden emotions running on constantly beneath the surface of your awareness, there's a stream of fleeting thoughts that runs right along with them. You probably rarely notice these little voices that keep your worries and fears alive. But these two covert streams of thought and feeling can combine to create a powerful and unpredictable force of nature. Like rogue waves, they can pop up when you least expect them and create havoc and uproar. Although these undercurrents of thought and feeling are hard to pinpoint, it's very important to know they're there so that you can slowly start to bring them to the surface where you can work with them.

RECOGNIZING TRIGGERS AND PATTERNS

After you've spent some time mindfully observing how you act and react while you're experiencing different emotional states, you'll start to see patterns. You'll be able to realize, *This is what my angry self looks like, my jealous self, my desire-filled self . . .* and so on. At that point, you'll have a pretty good snapshot of your emotional makeup. This fresh look at yourself under the influence of these habits can show you at what point in your pattern it's time to start heading for help—looking for an exit.

It's also important at this point to recognize what else might be going on around you that contributes to your reactions. While the deeper causes of our feelings aren't always clear, we can usually figure out the more immediate conditions that trigger an upsurge of emotional energy. Are there environmental or social conditions that typically influence you one way or another? What disturbs you, soothes you, puts you to sleep, or wakes you up?

Let's say you and your friend Joe head for your favorite beach one afternoon. The sun is shining and it's a perfect day. You're looking forward to spending time together in a serene natural setting. When you get there, you're disappointed to discover that the beach is crowded with families, joggers, body surfers, and sunbathers. Instead of relaxing, you get agitated. You quickly realize the sun is too hot and the water is too cold. You want to leave, but Joe feels fine and wants to stay. You start complaining, to no effect. So you start commenting on Joe's stubbornness ("so typical . . ."), which gets him going on how brilliant you are at getting your own way. Success—you ruined the day for yourself, your friend, and anyone nearby who had to listen to all the whining.

In this scenario, a little mindfulness could have changed the result. When you can recognize your frustrations just as they're starting up and see what's triggering them, that's what it means to see clearly. That kind of insight can save you from getting blindsided, tripping over yourself, or running into a wall—any of the usual ways you reach a painful point.

Usually we don't operate with such panoramic vision. When things start to get rocky, instead of taking a deep breath and looking around, you reach out for something to grab on to. You want your energy to have an anchor or clear focus. You tend to zero in on either yourself or the person (or thing) that upset you. When the spotlight falls on your own disturbed mind—if you're not paying attention, if you don't remember to be mindful—you fall into one of your old patterns. You inflict pain on yourself with your dizzying self-criticisms, and/or complaints about how hurt, humiliated, or burned up you feel. Whatever the pattern, it's all about what's happening to *me*, and that *me* becomes the central feature of the landscape. Everything else fades into the background.

The spotlight can also fall on the object of your emotions. If it's a person you're angry with—the dealer who sold you that lemon of a used car—then it's reasonable to feel some outrage at his scandalous behavior. But if you lose all mindfulness and get stuck there, that single-minded, narrow focus on one person can become an obsession. You mind gets caught in a groove, a pattern of recurring thoughts and feelings you can't shake. Then you're in trouble. Your focus isn't always a person, however. You can obsess over objects and ideas as well—the latest computer, losing ten pounds, or your side winning control of Congress.

STEADY AND FREE

What happens when you lose sight of the big picture and your narrow focus becomes obsessive? You fall into the trap of blame. Either you blame yourself or you blame others. Blame never results in good judgment, happiness, or wisdom. It only brings more confusion, more pain, and more ways of tying yourself into knots. You get more stuck, and freedom seems far away.

On the other hand, sometimes you can't seem to focus on anything at all. Your mind becomes like a camera in perpetual motion—when you try to focus on something, it just makes you dizzy. With practice, though, you become steadier. It gets easier to see the complete picture even under traumatic conditions.

The experience of Clear Seeing shows you the connection

between the inner world of your emotions and the world "out there." It shows you that you're not powerless when challenged by your own tendencies or external events. Instead of finding yourself bewildered, you can foresee how and where your emotions are likely to be triggered. You can predict when you might lose your mindfulness and become overwhelmed by intense feeling. At this point, it happens less and less. But if you feel yourself slipping, you remember what to do—you've regained your power in situations that used to make you lose it.

℘ ASK YOURSELF...
What pattern do my emotions follow?

You can use this set of questions to get a snapshot of any emotion that gives you trouble. Eventually you'll have a picture of your entire emotional being. When you can distinguish the emotions that need your immediate attention from those you can deal with later, it's easier to see where to focus your efforts in any given moment.

Substitute any emotion you want to evaluate as you ask yourself these questions:

◆ How often do I get *angry*? Once a day or once a week?

❖ When I get *angry*, what's the story I'm telling myself? For instance, "I get *angry* because . . ."

❖ When I do get *angry*, is my *anger* obvious to me, something I experience immediately and directly, or does it lurk in the background and gradually creep up on me?

❖ If the *anger* is strong, did it start off weak and gradually get more powerful? Or was it so powerful right at the beginning that I felt I had no control over it?

❖ How long does my *anger* typically last? Do I have any control over that? Can I get "un-mad" when I want to, or does my *anger* stay with me too long, like an unwelcome guest?

❖ Does my *anger* follow the same pattern as my other emotions?

You can answer most of these questions through simple, direct observation. As you contemplate, jot down your first thoughts or "doodle" your answers in quick little drawings. You can review them later. When you go back to them, ask yourself: Are they still accurate? Reflect further and add to them. Try spending one day focusing on a single question, for instance, "How do I get *angry*?" and another day focusing on the "story" that typically goes with that emotion.

5

A Sigh of Relief

When I let go of what I am,
I become what I might be.

—LAO-TZU

IF YOU REALLY want relief from your painful emotions, you have to be willing to kiss them good-bye. But before you can do that, you have to get to know them—to face their sharp edges and intense energies. Otherwise, you won't know what you're supposed to let go of.

The third step of the Emotional Rescue Plan is Letting Go, which should come as no surprise. It's the next logical step, the result of all the work you've done so far. You've already accomplished quite a lot through the Mindful Gap and Clear Seeing practices. You've learned different ways to work with intense emotional energy. You know how to create space between you and an emotion that's potentially overwhelming. And you've learned (or are learning) to spot the emotional triggers that set off those old "bad" habits—the ones you always regret while, at the same time, you still hang on to them. Learning those skills has shifted the way you look at your emotions. They are not bad through and through, after all. On the contrary, they are useful to you and full of positive potential. You see that Mindful Gap and Clear Seeing can free you from getting stuck in the same old dark and painful places. They guide you through the smoke and fire when you need a quick way out.

Now you're ready to work directly with the energy that fuels those emotional patterns. There's a saying that goes something like, *You have to let it come to let it go.* "Letting it come" happens through Mindful Gap, which then helps you to See Clearly, which in the end gives you the capacity to Let Go. But you're not just looking back, letting go, and saying a sentimental adios to your emotions. You're truly moving on, breathing easier, getting some real relief. But what are you "letting go" of—and how is this letting go different from rejecting or trying to get rid of your feelings?

On the one hand, you're letting go of your negative emotions—the feelings that cause you so much anxiety and grief. On the other, you're letting go of your habitual reactions to these intense feelings—trying to stop them, hide them, or change them. Once you're ready and willing to recognize your emotions as creative energy, Letting Go becomes merely a process of loosening the knots that your energy gets tied up in. An upsurge of energy gets tangled up when your habitual patterns get hold of it, hang on to it, and try to manipulate it in some way. When you get angry, for example, you have a choice: you can try to control it in the usual ways, or you can simply let the energy come and go. The tighter you hold on to energy that would otherwise move freely, the more you twist it this way and that, the tighter the knot, and the more anxiety and stress pervades your body and mind.

Step three, Letting Go, is about paying close attention to how you experience your emotions, both physically and mentally. The more attentive and aware you can be, the more power you'll have to release the bound-up energy. So Letting Go turns out to be the opposite of rejecting your emotions. It's actually the beginning of welcoming them into your life just as they are—original, fresh, creative energy that, if left to itself, moves on of its own accord. There's a burst of intensity when everything is wide open and full of possibility. Then you take your next breath.

GETTING MOTIVATED

It's easy to think, *I'm going to let go of these negative emotions. I really mean it!* But it's hard to do it. You have to be determined or it won't happen. So it helps to remind yourself of how destructive your neurotic way of relating to your emotions has been. Remember the negative impact it's had on your life and how it has hurt others, too.

What are the dangers of being engulfed by anger? Anger is like fire. It burns up your good qualities—destroys them in an instant. When you're hotheaded, boiling mad, inflamed, you risk turning into someone you don't even recognize. You lose your common sense and might do or say something you would never have imagined saying or doing. A bitter comment, a shouting match, or a slap, and you've destroyed a relationship you've nurtured with patience and diligence for years.

If that weren't enough, anger also spoils your appearance. No matter how well dressed and presentable you think you are, the moment you become aggressive, no one sees your beauty. Your fine clothes, cool gear, and stylish makeup? Suddenly none of it makes a difference. You lose not just your impressive physical appearance, but the beauty of your mind and good heart.

Of all the emotions, anger is the most destructive. Yet each one brings its own brand of pain and struggle. Too much desire and we're filled with a hunger that robs us of our ability to enjoy what we're so desperate to possess. When we're jealous, we're always a little paranoid, always struggling to outdo the "competition," which could be anybody! We envy the talents of others and resent the success of our rivals. When we're inflated with pride, we feel superior to others. We're above the competition, self-absorbed, and not a lot of help to all those "below" us, whom we hardly notice. These mind states can take us over for mere moments, or they can become marks of our personal style, like the clothes we wear or the car we drive. And even though one emotion by itself may not be purely negative, it can trigger other emotions, causing a chain reaction.

When at last we understand the destructive potential of disturbing emotions on a deeply personal level, we might be motivated to try something new: letting go of these feelings instead of holding on to them. If we don't like the outcome, we can always go back to our former neurotic habits. They will definitely still be there. We don't need to worry about losing them overnight.

You can test this crazy "letting go" idea in a few small, simple ways. If you always do the same thing, like ordering only hamburgers in restaurants, going only to action movies, or never leaving the house without your cell phone, try something different. Order a chimichanga, go see a play, and leave your phone at home when you go out. See how you feel. Even such small steps can be liberating.

In the same way, you can at least try letting go of a budding resentment when all your instincts are saying you really need to hang on to it. Just try it out and see how it feels. You can tell yourself, *I'm going to give this a fair shot. The next time I'm freaked out, I'm going to remember the ER Plan. I'm going to Mind the Gap, and then try to See Clearly—and start learning to relax and Let Go.*

That's a good start, but it's important to know, too, that it's not possible to release 100 percent of your negative emotions right away. If you expect to release them all at once, you'll be disappointed because that's never going to happen. But it's not all bad news. The good news is that you can reach your goal, not all at once, but by degrees.

The first time you try letting go of a destructive emotion like anger, you'll be able to release at least some of its energy. The next time it turns up, you can release a little more. Then, on the third try, you can release even more of what remains. Each time you let go of the anger, what remains is just a little less intense, and each time the emotion comes back, it's in reduced form—it's less imposing and more manageable. As you apply this step, over time your reactivity starts to dissipate (like letting air out of a balloon) and the emotion becomes more workable, which is a good and achievable goal.

Even after some time, however, no matter how much effort you've put into it, there will be a residue of the anger left behind. At this stage, the emotional energy that remains with you is like the scent that lingers when a perfume bottle is emptied. In the same way, even though an emotion may be virtually gone, some telltale sign of its energy remains a while longer in the form of a basic tendency. It's like giving up drinking coffee or smoking cigarettes. Once you've gone beyond the craving stage, there's still an occasional flicker of desire or impulse in that direction, but no longer any basis to act on it.

Letting go of your negative emotions takes place on two levels. First, you gradually release the most apparent energy of the emotion. Once you're skilled in that, you can work at letting go on a more subtle level, so that even the scent left behind fades away. This process takes time and effort, but it frees you of the direct pain of those emotions as well as their disturbing undercurrents.

LETTING GO: SEE, HEAR, SMELL, TASTE, TOUCH

Step three of the ER Plan, Letting Go, begins with being present and observant just as in the previous steps. There's a sense of being "here," wherever you are—in your room or at the mall. If your mind is wandering, time-traveling, or daydreaming, you come down to earth. You bring your attention to the present moment and place.

Then, as soon as you're aware of the presence of an emotion, try to connect with the physical world around you instead of focusing on your strong feelings and racing thoughts. You do this by shifting your attention to what your senses are registering. Ask yourself: *What are my eyes seeing? What are my ears hearing? What odors or tastes do I notice? What sensations do I feel?* Take a moment to notice the coolness of a breeze, the warmth of the sun, or the hardness or softness of your chair.

It's enough just to connect with that experience. There's no need to do anything else but focus briefly on a single sense object—a sound, a visual form—without adding anything extra to the experience. You don't need to think about it, or label it, or judge it. When a thought comes up, that's fine, but don't pursue it. Let it go and return to your simple focus.

It's a lot like being an investigative reporter. If you're a good journalist, you just observe the situation and then write about it. You don't interfere with the story. You don't ask leading questions. You don't look for answers that confirm what you think you already know. You keep an open, unbiased, watchful mind. That's the job description. There's no need to do anything else.

When you begin directing your attention to your sensory experience, two things happen. Your agitation begins to settle down and you feel calmer. At the same time, you interrupt the momentum of the emotion's energy, which helps you create the Mindful Gap experience. And that's what you're looking for and trying to connect with at first—the gap that can buy you some time, maybe even preventing a negative emotion from bursting into full bloom.

What's more, connecting with your sensory experience helps to relax your mind. There's a sense of simply being in the present moment. It can be a kind of meditation. When you use your sense perceptions in this way, they're like shock absorbers in a car that has just hit a pothole in the road—the senses absorb some of the impact of your emotions so that you don't suffer quite so much.

LETTING GO: RELAX YOUR BODY

Once you've connected with your sense perceptions, the next thing you do is connect with your body. When you're overwhelmed by an emotion, you usually forget all about your body. So here you bring your attention to your physical self, but very simply, without thinking about it too much. Simply let yourself feel the energy of emotion in your body. Beyond that, you don't add anything onto the experience. You don't need to become self-conscious and think, *Oh this is a good body*, or *This is a terrible body*, or that it's healthy or unhealthy or whatever thoughts you usually have about your body. Try to drop all those thoughts, labels, and judgments, and just feel what it feels like to be in your body. Rest in that experience and allow any emotional disturbance to settle down and relax.

When you connect with your body in such a direct, simple, and nonconceptual way, you start to relax. Physical relaxation not only helps you see your emotions more clearly, it also helps you release intense emotional energy. Most of the time, we're not really here, in our body. We only know our body through the labels we give it. We put on a mask of labels and when we look in a mirror, we see that mask: beautiful, ugly, pleasant, unpleasant, and so on. It's a mask of concepts, a mask of judgments. We scare ourselves, because we forget we're wearing a mask. In a way, we never actually see behind the disguise (our labels). We never really see our body in its ordinary, mundane form—just as it is, unembellished by thoughts.

When you can drop all your labels and simply look at your body without judgment, you have a completely different experience of your body. You start to see your true self, your true body behind the mask. It's a profound insight that brings a sense of peace and a much more optimistic outlook. You're no longer so identified with all those concepts and disturbing emotions related to your body. You can see through the confusion that comes from these labels and judgments. If you can remember to be mindful of your body when you're upset or anxious, your physical awareness can pull you back from the brink just in time.

No matter what emotion strikes, you can feel it in your body and then let go and relax with the breath. Remember that one of the easiest ways to release emotional energy in the body is to take a few deep breaths. Just one cycle of deep breathing can make a big difference when you need to physically release an emotion.

Certain kinds of physical exercise such as yoga and swimming can be beneficial, too. Yoga helps to improve the flow of energy in your body and it can alleviate tension caused by strong emotions. If you're not able to do these sorts of exercises, you can practice mindfulness of body while sitting quietly indoors, while lying down outside looking up at the sky, or while walking in a park. You also can do it while washing dishes or watching TV. When you need to let go of emotional disturbances, the practice of meditation can be especially helpful. Although we tend to think of meditation as being only a mental practice, it's also physical. It works with both the breath and our physical posture. (Detailed instructions for meditation are included on pages 133–37 in the section "Exercises and Pointers.")

When you do any of these things—whether you're exercising, doing yoga, meditating, or simply remembering to pause a moment, breathe, and relax—it's important to continue to stay mindful and aware of your experiences of both your body and your mind. While releasing emotional energy tied up in the body, stay connected to your experience of mind. Otherwise, physical exercise just becomes another way of distracting yourself from your emotions. That's not letting go of your emotions; it's a way of avoiding them, keeping them at a distance. To let go of something, you first have to be close enough to get ahold of it.

Letting Go: Relax Your Mind

The next step is to release the emotion mentally. Just as you did when relaxing your body, observe the experience of your emotional mind like a good reporter. When you notice that an emotion is bothering you, simply identify it and let yourself experience its energy. According to recent research in the fields of psychology and neuroscience, just the act of naming an emotion, calling it "anger" or "sadness" or "worry," is enough to decrease its intensity. That gives you a chance to get a better look at it. The label isn't intended to make things more elaborate or complicated. You're just telling yourself what the emotion is: *Right now I'm angry.* Don't expand on that with further thoughts like, *This is good anger*; *This is bad anger*; or *I need to stop this anger*; etc. In other words, don't add any blah blah blah.

Once you've identified the feeling, just look at its qualities and how it's getting expressed. If it's passion, are you agitated? Are your thoughts racing? What message is your passion sending? What's your response to that message? Whatever's happening, simply feel it, be aware of it, and acknowledge it. You don't have to figure it out all at once. Just look at each emotion as it comes up; watch it; be very aware of your experience.

Once it's clear what the emotion is—no more labeling! Don't hold on to it with your thoughts. The more labels you apply, the more elaborate the story line grows and the more attached to it you become. The gap between you and your emotion gets smaller and smaller, and your emotional mind gets more agitated and confused.

Instead just let it be. That's another way to describe Letting Go. When an emotion pops up, let it come. When it changes, let it change. And when it goes, let it go. Let it dissolve into open space. When that happens, instead of feeling blank or empty, you may feel a sigh of relief and a vivid sense of your own presence.

This process requires time and patience, and it's fine to go slowly. But at some point, you'll need to deal with your hidden emotions as well. How do you let go of feelings you've repressed? Before you can let them go, you have to find them and get a good look at what they are. When you open the door to looking into your repressed feelings, it's like walking into a crowded room, looking for someone you don't know very well. When you look inside, there are a bunch of emotions and thoughts just humming along, talking, arguing, doing what they do, and at first it's hard to see the ones you're looking for. They are quite shy and won't reveal themselves or their secrets so easily. But you'll still need to find a way to make contact and approach them. You can begin to draw them out by asking yourself some questions like, *Are there certain emotions I especially want to avoid? What do I do to keep from feeling them? Am I suppressing any emotions right now?*

Eventually you'll be able to look back into the past to see if you can learn more—which emotions you've been trying to avoid and when and how they started. In time, you'll understand more about who you are. You'll come to appreciate the intelligence and bravery that's led you to this moment of discovery.

LET GO OF THE LET-GOER

When you reach this level of Letting Go, there's just one final thing you need to do: let go of the "let-goer." That means you can relax even further. Now you can let go of all the extra effort of tracking yourself. You can give up your preoccupation with "me," the one who created all those mindful gaps, learned to see so clearly, and finally, bravely, let go of those disturbing emotions.

When you're free of fixation on the idea, *I am the one who is letting go*, you'll be transforming your emotions at a very subtle level. You're relaxing the part of you that's been so keenly judging you and vigilantly watching you watch your emotions. It's the double agent of awareness, the self-aware watcher and performer of all the things you say and do.

When you can relax this deeply, you see how getting all knotted up in neurotic emotional patterns is like tying a snake into a knot. If you let go of the snake, it easily unknots itself. The only way to keep the knot tied is to keep holding on to the snake. In the same way, once you decide to let go of an emotion that's reached a painful point, the pure energy of that emotion will naturally unknot itself—because, ultimately, emotions come and go on their own. There is no one who "frees you" from your emotions—not even you.

At the same time, there is no one else but you who can make this discovery for yourself. And no one but you can make up your mind to transform how you relate to your emotions. So at this point you come face-to-face with a question: *Am I willing to let this knot come untied?*

ᴥ Ask yourself...
How do I feel emotion in my body?

When you feel the clear presence of an emotion, try following this instruction.

Whatever the emotion is, direct your attention to your whole body, your basic physical presence, and then begin to scan your body from bottom to top: soles of feet to the crown of your head, or move inward from fingers and toes to your heart center. The point is to notice where you feel the effects of the emotion and what those effects are. Negative emotions can provoke a wide range of physical symptoms. Look carefully again and again to see what the signs are and if they change:

* *Am I tense? Where is the tension located?*
* *Is my breathing shallow or rapid?*
* *Am I trembling or shaky? Is my face flushed?*
* *Do I feel any distress—a tightness in my chest or pounding in my head?*

Once you've observed your physical state, there are a number of things you can do to help you relax and release the energy pent up in your body. For example, if you feel your jaw clenching, bring your awareness to that spot and breathe in and out deeply, consciously bringing a sense of openness and relaxation to that place.

Letting Go with the Breath

- Think of a time in the recent past when you were irritated and upset.
- Connect with that moment until you begin to sense the emotions that came up for you then.
- Now inhale deeply, focusing your mind on the breath and relaxing your body. Don't rush to exhale. Lightly hold the breath for just a moment, and then let it go.
- Repeat this a few times, and notice any change in your experience.

6

Thoughts and Emotions

*Few are those who see with their own eyes
and feel with their own hearts.*

—ALBERT EINSTEIN

IF YOU'VE MADE it to this point, you've learned the basics of
the ER Plan and you've started to put the three steps into
practice. You've come a long way. Now you understand a
great deal about your emotions and about how to free yourself from the push and pull of your habitual tendencies.
That's the complete package. You have the method, and you
know why and how it should work for you. We could skip
now to the happy ending—how your discovery of your
emotions as creative energy opens your life to new possibilities while all your problems dissolve. As the English poet
Lord Byron sang, "On with the dance! Let joy be uncon-
fined."

Before going there, however, let's take a closer look at
how your thoughts and emotions work together and the part
that labeling plays in that partnership. In a sense, this is like

a "lab" session concentrating on the use of one of your primary tools: mindfulness. The more skillful you are with this tool, the more you can see—of how you think, feel, and act—at peace or under fire. It's like looking through a high-quality microscope onto the surface of a high-quality mirror.

It isn't enough just to read books and studies put out by experts. If you're ever going to know your emotions as they truly are, you have to test your assumptions and see what happens. When your emotions are just dawning—when they're alive and full of juice—go right out to meet them. Look at what you do when you're "tested": What happens if you lose your job, get the flu on vacation, or your best friend moves far away? Do you completely crash, or try to cheer yourself up by making everyone else miserable? Your actions are more likely to be timely and appropriate when they're based on direct experience, not speculation or imagination—not on *maybe's* or *what-if's*.

Your Mind Says "Rose"

If you look at your thoughts closely, and keep looking at them, you'll notice something that occurs regularly. Whenever you see something, your mind instantly produces a label for it. You could be looking at an actual three-dimensional object, like a rose, or you could be picturing a purely mental object, like a memory of a rose you once gave to your sweetheart on Valentine's Day. Either way, your mind says "rose" when that object appears to it (to your mind, that is).

At the most basic level, all our labels are just thoughts, simple concepts: *flower, table, iPod, Susie, Rover.* Everything gets its own name or tag. Sometimes you think of it, and sometimes you learn it. It's "common knowledge," part of your culture and language. But on top of that basic label, you quickly add thoughts that say more: *good, bad, right, wrong,* etc. Soon, you're labeling *friends* and *enemies,* making judgments, planning your next party, and eventually your life, around these concepts. Your labels become so talkative that they weave together a compelling story. And you're so moved by the story that you start to forget the part you played in creating it.

For example, you might meet somebody and think to yourself, *My new neighbor, Sam, is a nice guy—a really good person.* Now you have the label *good.* Then there is Sam, who has no idea what you're thinking. Sam has physical attributes you can see: he's tall, thin, wears glasses, and has short brown hair. But where is the thing that says *good?* It's not a sign stuck on Sam's forehead. *Good* is just your own thought, which for some reason was triggered when you first met Sam.

What happens when you create such a label? You mix together the actual person, Sam, and your notion of good. The distinction between the two becomes blurred. The next time you see Sam, you automatically think *good person* again. Suddenly the distinction between *good* and *the person*

Sam is gone. Your new neighbor is now stamped with that label. Imagine your surprise when one day you discover Sam doing something bad, like stealing money, or beating his dog. You might suffer an existential crisis. How can a good person do bad things? If you now call Sam *bad*, however, you're just trading one label for another, and it doesn't clarify anything. You're only creating a new label, imposing it on Sam, and thinking that's reality.

Consider the labels you create every day. To what degree do you think they influence you? Our labels always seem to affect how we treat someone, how we talk about them, how we view their friends, possessions, accomplishments, and so on. And we do this equally to ourselves. Some labels are more accurate than others, of course, but when events contradict our expectations, we get upset. We may become completely overwhelmed and have difficulty handling the situation—all because our label and the thing we were labeling didn't quite match up.

For this reason, when we're working with our emotions, it's important to loosen our labels, or relax our attachment to them. Instead of assuming they're valid, we can get in the habit of questioning them. We don't have to give our labels special status just for showing up in our minds. Whether these notions have occurred to us only once, or a thousand times, doesn't matter. It's important to notice the power that our labels exert over us and how that power reverberates throughout our lives and across our communities.

༄ HOW DO MY EMOTIONS CHANGE?

(Include any emotion you want to evaluate.)

❖ What do I notice first when I become *angry*?

❖ When I identify *anger* and label it, what happens?

❖ Does labeling the feeling change how I experience it?

❖ If so, what changes? The emotion itself, or my perception of it?

❖ How do I know when the anger has dissolved?

Since all of this takes place in your mind, you're in a perfect position to check it out at any time. You only need to stop what you're doing for a few minutes and take a look. Setting aside just fifteen minutes a day to slow down and contemplate such questions can go a long way toward bringing relief and clarity to troubling situations. Don't worry if the answers don't come easily at first. The most important thing is to practice looking. As you keep at it, it will get easier.

LETTING GO OF LABELS

By looking at how your thoughts and your labeling mind work, you begin to see beyond the surface of your emotions. You see that projecting labels onto people and things removes you from direct experience. It creates a kind of buffer zone between you and your world. You never really have to get to know Sam, or let him get to know you. You have each other pegged. (Don't forget, he's got a label for you, too.) When this tendency goes too far we find ourselves isolated, cut off from others, and cut off from our own creative energy.

To recover a sense of direct experience and reconnect with your vital energy, you need to go beyond your labels. Your labeled emotions are like processed junk foods—full of artificial flavors and colors. They may be more palatable than your raw, unprocessed emotions, but their empty calories are a lot less nourishing. Fortunately, emotions can't really be processed like our food. Their essence always remains just what it is. So in any given moment, you can reconnect with a fresh experience of emotion.

By doing a little probing, you can find out more about the original feeling. You notice that when this emotion first arrives, it's naked. It shows up without any label to tell you what it is. There's no pop-up window that reads, "I am anger" or "I am passion" or "I am something good." It's just an experience of pure energy, like the innocent energy of a small child. Sometimes that energy rests peacefully and wakes up smiling—but a moment later it can be shouting and bouncing off the walls.

If you don't know what it's about or how to deal with it directly, at least you can try to contain it. It's what you might do with a roomful of noisy children—contain the energy by pulling out the toys or turning on the cartoon channel.

In a similar way, we divert the energy of our raw emotions into our conceptualized versions. As soon as this naked feeling appears, we label it, and it subtly changes. When our emotions are infiltrated by labels, they feel a bit "off." They take on the qualities of our superimposed concepts and begin to feel contrived or made up. Whatever feeling it is, it's no longer the pure, unadulterated version we first met with. The difference between these two—the original feeling and the labeled feeling—is like the difference between original Coke and Cherry Coke. Sure, they're both Coke, but they aren't the same. To get Cherry Coke, you have to change the taste of original Coke; it's no longer the original thing. We should always go for the real thing—the original emotion—not the Cherry Coke version.

℘ Do my emotions change what I think?

* Do I attribute different qualities to someone when I'm angry/jealous/passionate?
* How many of the qualities I see in a person really belong to that person, and how many are just my projections? For example, one day you think your brother-in-law (or your stockbroker) is a great guy looking out for your interests, and the next week he's a self-serving idiot!
* Does being angry or happy change what I think of myself?

Reflect on it

Contemplate these questions and then write for five or ten minutes in response to each one. You could respond to all three in one sitting, or you might choose one per day for several days.

Option

Contemplate each question, and then respond in 140 characters—a tweet (to yourself).

If your concepts and labels matched up with the way things really are, then everything would be fine. But that's not how it is. Because there's a disparity between what you're telling yourself and what's actually occurring, you get confused. You may even think your projections make perfect sense, but in the end that isn't the point. If you want to understand your emotional experience, if you want a lasting solution to your persistent struggle, you need to let go of your labels (or at least let go of your blind faith in them). Your emotions only reveal their beautiful, natural wisdom when you leave them just as they are, without any artificial additives.

GENERATIONS OF CONFUSION

Here's how we get confused. From our initial mixing up of our labeling thoughts and the things we stick them onto—the red rose or our neighbor Sam—we create our first generation of misunderstandings. From that jumble arises a second generation of emotions and a second generation of labels. And this process repeats itself over and over again. The second generation becomes the basis for a third, and it all becomes very complicated. If you look at your original experience and compare it to what you end up with several generations later, the two don't resemble each other at all. In the end, you may still be struggling with a difficult emotion, but you're no closer to understanding it. You're not really in touch with your true feelings, and you're not even sure what the conflict was all about in the first place.

In Sichuan Province in China, there's a marketplace that is famous for the arguments that go on there. When a dispute between two people breaks out, inevitably a couple of people in the crowd will take sides, even though they don't know what the argument is about. They'll start fighting with each other and keep it up even after the original two have gotten tired and gone home. The arguing spreads, with more and more people choosing sides, yelling at each other and waving their arms around. So the argument continues even after the second two have gone away. The fighting can go on for quite a while with no one having any idea who or what started it all.

Our emotions play out just like this. But we don't recognize it. We think it's all the same—one uninterrupted stream of stubbornness or malice—from start to finish, no matter how long it goes on or how many voices have added their two cents from the sidelines. Until we've worked with our emotions and can see through some of this deception, our labels and concepts continue to perpetuate confusion.

When you get a good look at all this, you realize these labels aren't helping you at all, and that it's futile to rely on them. The exception to this is that first thought that arises immediately with your emotion. For example, if you have a fresh experience of anger, and you're able to give it a conceptual label (*I'm angry now*), in this case, identifying the emotion can help you let go of it before it becomes unmanageable. Quick, straightforward thoughts like these help you clarify your emotions and understand them. But if you allow your thoughts to run wild and pile up on top of each other, you'll lose your connection to the original emotion and fall back into confusion.

Breaking free of these basic tendencies happens gradually. Don't expect that you'll be able to do it perfectly right away. You'll be transforming your attitude and approach to your emotions as you go through each stage. Of course, from the beginning you can adopt the idea that emotions are actually creative energy, and not just worthless garbage or cast-off goods that might be worth recycling. But this is only a nice theory, an intellectual notion, until you bring it into your personal experience. It takes time, but the investment of that time will yield a big return. If you stick with it, you'll be surprised at how much calmer and steadier you are in situations that used to throw you off balance.

There's a wonderful side benefit, too. The more you become able to see emotions as they really are, the easier it is to connect with your basic heart of kindness.

๑ ASK YOURSELF...

How do my thoughts and feelings interact?

If you've practiced meditation, you may be familiar with the technique of recognizing the presence of thoughts. It's a simple practice and an effective way to sharpen your mindfulness. All you have to do is watch your mind and notice any thoughts that arise. When you recognize the presence of a thought, you say to yourself, *Thinking*, then you let the thought go and return to a sense of watchfulness.

When you extend this practice of identifying thoughts to working with active emotions, you watch the contents of your mind in the same way. Only now you're watching for both thoughts and emotions. The point, however, is not just to identify the thoughts and emotions that pass through your mind—to tag them the way you might tag photos on your Facebook page. As helpful as this is in standard meditation practices, you're doing something slightly different here. You're watching not only for the presence of thoughts and emotions in your mind, *but also to see how your thoughts and feelings interact. How do your emotions and thoughts communicate with each other and influence each other?*

To practice this kind of "thought inspection," set aside

a little time to quietly observe your mind. It's best to have a comfortable seat and to sit with an upright but relaxed posture. It's helpful to begin with a positive state of mind, which could simply mean thinking a positive thought or making an uplifting wish or aspiration.

Once you're sitting comfortably, relax your mind and observe the coming and going of your thoughts without trying to change them. When a thought appears to your mind, label it minimally while noticing its content and qualities. (*Oh, that's anxiety. I'm thinking about that job interview again. It's like a pounding inside my head.*) It's important to keep the labeling simple and to remain mindful and alert. Basically, you're not doing anything but getting familiar with the way your mind works.

After doing this for a while, you can take a step back and look at your thought process in general. You can ask yourself questions and explore your emotional journey from the moment that an emotion first arises to the moment when you attach your labels to it.

You'll find more detailed instructions for practicing observing your thoughts in "Catching Your Thoughts" on page 136, in Part Two of this book.

7

An Unexpected Gift

*Kindness is the language which the deaf
can hear and the blind can see.*

—MARK TWAIN

WHEN I WAS just a boy, I received an unexpected gift of a snake from one of my teachers. The snake was long and bright green, with red markings shaped like four-petaled flowers on her back. Very beautiful. She was delivered in a glass box by a friend. First I was told, "Be careful when you feed her. She's a poisonous snake, you know."

My face must have turned very pale, because then he added, "Don't worry, they took out the venom, so there's no poison anymore. You still have to be careful, though. It's a very aggressive type of snake. Look what happened to me." My friend then showed me a big scar on the palm of his hand. When I asked what I should feed her, he gave me a packet of powder from India, some chickpea flour or something, which I was supposed to mix with milk. He explained how I was to open the box, pick up the snake, take her out, and feed her. I said, "Oh, thank you very much." What choice did I have? My teacher sent it to me to take care of! But I was really terrified of this snake.

When I took it home, my mom was upset, but she had great respect for my teacher and couldn't really get mad at him. The whole family was quite excited at their first sight of the snake in my room. For a long time, whenever I put my hand in to try to pull out the snake and feed her, she would try to bite me. Every single time. It took me a while to create a good relationship with the snake. Gradually, though, I learned how to put my hand out in such a way that it didn't agitate or threaten her. Then I could just pick her up. After I learned this, she was very gentle.

Just as I needed to develop a kind of rapport with that poisonous snake in order to feed and care for her every day, we need to feel a sympathetic connection with even our scary and difficult emotions. What we're doing with the Three-Step ER Plan isn't just a technical project—learning how to do this and that so we don't screw up. We're trying to find a way to relieve the pain and suffering we go through because of these emotions. When we're dealing with feelings that can hurt us—that can startle and threaten and bite—we need to do more than just be cautious. We need to care about ourselves, too, and what we're going through. We can give ourselves a little love and compassion, especially in hard times. Of course, we think of others, too, but we won't have much compassion to give others if we're not being kind to ourselves.

IT'S ALL RIGHT TO BE YOU

When you're in risky emotional territory, there's nothing more important than being kind to yourself. True kindness is always welcome. You can count on it to bring positive results—a frown instantly becomes a smile. Being kind is like being polite in the best sense of the word. It's how we act to make another person feel comfortable, at home, and fundamentally respected. It's sincere and heartfelt, merciful and gracious. When you're engaged in a challenging project like working with your difficult emotions, remember to show yourself a little bit of kindness, too.

That means having some sympathy and appreciation for your day-to-day life and struggles. It means giving yourself a break while you're trying your best to change the way you deal with your emotions. If you're still approaching your emotions like enemies on a battlefield, how will you be able to appreciate their creative play or discover their wisdom? What you're doing here is simple, but it isn't going to be easy. It's going to take a lot of effort over time. So you can acknowledge your willingness to go for it, to stick with it. You can give yourself a pat on the back. The whole process will work much better if you relax and take it easy.

When you think about it, kindness is always relaxed. Of course, there are exceptions. There are times when the kindest thing we can do is to help someone face an uncomfortable truth. Or look in the mirror and face our own reflection without blinders. Kindness is not always about saying yes or giving out compliments. But in whatever way it's expressed, kindness never undermines or denigrates. Its message is always, *Whatever you're going through right now, it's all right to be you—to be who you are.*

Don't worry about how your emotions compare to someone else's. You can't tell anyway, because everyone's unique. We're all neurotic in our own ways. What really matters is your own experience and what you think. You have to be honest with yourself. But no matter how difficult your situation seems to you, it's who you are, and you have to deal with it. No one else can do it for you. No one else can be you, with the particular emotional challenges you face. But that's all right. Everyone has their own weird trips, worries, and crazy thoughts. Your baggage isn't better or worse, it's just yours. It's what you have to work with, so whoever you are is fine.

The end result of working with your emotions might just be that realization: it's all right to be you. There doesn't need to be a new, improved model of you. Despite all your emotional turmoil and slipups, your true self doesn't need to be debugged, reprogrammed, or replaced. As you work to change the habitual patterns that keep you locked up in suffering and confusion, remember that those patterns aren't you. Those patterns aren't the true nature of your emotions, either. They're a kind of temporary identity you take on—the angry boss, the jealous boyfriend, the overanxious parent. But behind whatever masks you may wear, there is a tremendous source of wisdom, power, and energy. Because this is so, you can always recover the creative energy, happiness, and joy that you've lost, or abandoned, or just stopped seeing.

What happens after you've "rescued" and recovered yourself? What do you do with all of the creative energy you've liberated from the grip of your habitual patterns? What makes it worth the time and commitment it's taken you to get here?

YOUR LIFE UNOBSTRUCTED

When you start to develop a clear and honest relationship with your emotions, you're not only getting to know your feelings better—you're also getting to know who *you* are. The further you can go with the practices of Mindful Gap, Clear Seeing, and Letting Go, the closer you are to recognizing that your emotions—freed from your anxieties, fears, and labels—are the energetic expression of your vast human potential for happiness, creativity, and compassion.

That's how it was when I learned to take care of my pet snake. At first I was nervous about handling her because she was always trying to bite me. I finally realized that the more I relaxed around her, the more she seemed to relax around me, too. Once I learned to approach her without a lot of worry, we both had a better time of it. At that point I began to see what a beautiful creature she was—and what an amazing gift had fallen into my hands.

When you can simply let them be in their natural state, your emotions are like a brilliant work of art; the more you look, the more there is to see. They attract us with their color, energy, and movement, and sometimes with their utter silence. They touch us on a level beyond words. They link us to a deep, universal source of meaning and fulfillment.

We can find demonstrations of inspired vision and authentic feeling throughout the arts. But such gifts often seem to reside "out there," within the rarefied walls or DNA of superhuman beings we label "artists." We don't really believe that we possess the same brilliance. How could we? But discovering the power of your emotions is something like finding your "inner fire" and learning how to use it well. Instead of feeling powerless and deprived, it's possible to feel at ease and move through your life with grace and dignity.

When you're free of the handicap of your habitual tendencies (and the burden of negative emotions), you're free to develop who *you* are. The energy that once inhibited you can now carry you forward. Whatever you choose to do, you can do it with less suffering, less fear, and less confusion about why things happen the way they do.

Realizing the potential of your "rescued" creative energy means that you can appreciate, explore, and find new expressions for your own unique experiences and talents.

You're free to discover your pure passions, and your own heartfelt vision for a meaningful and productive life. This doesn't mean that suddenly "we are all artists" and thus sweeping the floor and doing the laundry instantly become works of art. These ordinary tasks can be done artfully and with mindfulness, of course. But it's more about having a mind that's bright and clear, with positive qualities of attention that give you better vision, that help you see those sparks of beauty and richness throughout your life and all around you. No part of this picture is insignificant. Every aspect is a meaningful part of the whole.

THE LIVES OF OTHERS

Seeing the whole picture can be a cumulative process, like walking a far distance one step at a time, or it can happen in a single flash of mindfulness. You see this moment, this step, and also the world you're passing through. And you notice how you're linked to everything you see. The more clearly you perceive this, the more you understand that all of your actions have a direct impact on this world. There are always consequences. Hurtful words and actions have a ripple effect. The harm they do extends far beyond the point of impact. In the same way, kind words and deeds spread a positive and uplifting message farther than the eye can see.

Paying attention to the impact of your actions is a way to begin developing sympathy for others. Because you start to see their struggles so sharply, you naturally feel compassion, which means "to suffer with." Compassion isn't a mild, generalized feeling of, *Gosh, isn't that a shame?* It's a powerful and compelling response to the suffering of others that wants to ease that suffering. It's passionate and unselfish, and it comes with a sense of commitment to act, not just feel. It carries you out of emotional seclusion into the messy, joyful world of relationship.

But to develop that kind of pure love toward others, you need to have the same love and compassionate concern for yourself and your own well-being. So, whether you're talking about yourself or others, kindness always applies. It can help defuse explosive emotions and strengthen positive ones. It helps you feel happier, safer, and in greater control of your life. And that helps you develop peace of mind as well as peace on the streets of your neighborhood.

Being kind doesn't attract much attention. It won't land you on TV or lead to fame and fortune. As we normally think of it, kindness is a nice quality, but not an exceptional one, like bravery or heroism. We assume anyone can be kind, even very young children. But to be truly kind aligns us with the principles of nonviolence. We have to think about it and make a courageous decision to live without harming anyone, no matter what. That's a very rare, mature, and selfless view. Sometimes it means we simply stop ourselves from doing something hurtful, which is a potent action in itself. But at other times, an act of kindness can be transformative. It can change a bad mood to a good one or a destructive impulse into a selfless gesture of friendship. Instead of a slap in the face, a handshake. Instead of an enemy, a friend.

You can cultivate an attitude of kindness in two ways: first, by holding the intention to not harm anyone—including yourself; and, second, by holding the intention to make all your actions positive ones, which takes it a little further. This doesn't mean just stopping yourself from inflicting distress or pain, but sincerely trying to make all your actions (physical, verbal, and mental) constructive and helpful. Try it out for twenty-four hours and see what happens. Find out what it feels like to be free of the burden of negativity, whatever that is for you. Most of us carry around more negativity than we'd like (or than we realize). If you drop it for twenty-four hours, you might find yourself genuinely relaxing and thoroughly enjoying a whole day and night.

The catch is that we're not pretending here. It's not a game where the winner is the person with the nicest smile and the prettiest words. We're trying to connect with our deepest heart of kindness, to find a way to feel optimistic about our life and bring a little joy into the world. Of course, you can't expect to be 100 percent positive for twenty-four hours straight, but you can aim high and see how far you can reach. If you can make an honest effort to do these two things—remain kind, and stay positive—you gain an inner power and freedom that shines through all of your actions and grows stronger with time.

TWENTY-FOUR HOURS OF KINDNESS

For this experiment to work, you need to commit to it. Tell yourself you won't give in to the same old habits. You won't pull out your verbal guns and start firing right away. You'll pause, take a few minutes, and remember that (a) you have a choice, and (b) whatever you decide will have consequences. If you don't stop and think before acting or speaking, afterward you might end up telling yourself, *Oh no! I didn't mean to say that, but now I'm going to have to pay for it.* There are some things we can't take back. All our remorse and apologies may not restore a broken relationship or keep us out of court.

This isn't to say you shouldn't express yourself—just try not to harm anyone (or undermine yourself) in the process. If you can extend a little kindness all around, you're likely to be more open, and the other guy's likely to be more receptive. Then, instead of getting swallowed up in a recurring nightmare, you're in a fresh, clear space, where communication is possible.

We all want to escape the nightmares that plague us, so that we can fulfill our dream of changing our life and turning it in a more positive direction. We long to feel the simple joy of living, instead of just suppressing our fear and pain. So how about trying to live that dream? Even imagining it can cheer us up for a while. We won't succeed every minute, but we may succeed for a day. If we don't try, we'll never know what we can accomplish. That's just good, old-fashioned common sense.

ᕲ ASK YOURSELF . . .

How does a positive or negative attitude
affect my emotions?

To see how your attitude can affect your emotions, try out
this simple exercise at home or at work.

1. For a single day, try to maintain a positive, optimistic attitude: hold the intention to not cause any un-
   necessary pain, distress, or confusion of any kind,
   for yourself or anyone else.

   ❖ Try making a written agreement with yourself
     to do this. You might put it in a box near your
     bedside.

   If you fall short at any time during the day, that's fine.
   Don't dwell on it. Take a deep breath, and just return to
   your positive intention.

2. At the end of the day before going to sleep, look
   back at your actions and reflect on what happened.
   Ask yourself:

   ❖ How much of the day was I able to sustain a
     positive attitude?

❖ How often did my attitude change?

❖ When I lost it (and felt a little cynical or pessimistic), did my emotions change?

❖ Did I notice any difference in how I spoke to people or in people's reactions to me?

❖ Make notes that you can review later.

If the exercise seems too simple, try it anyway once or twice. Sometimes your thoughts will try to talk you out of making changes—that's actually an indication what you're doing is having an effect.

When you're trying this out—trying to keep yourself positive—it may help to remember that before you do or say something, there's already a thought in your mind. Before you tip the barista, for instance, you're thinking, *One dollar.* Before you compliment or shout at your soon-to-be mother-in-law, your thoughts are already flattering her or yelling at her. So, throughout the day, look at your thoughts before you act. The bold ones are easy to spot, but check for the ones that are more hidden, too. You know what mischief they can cause.

This exercise is intended to boost your awareness of unhelpful and often unconscious habits, and gradually introduce more positive alternatives. If a whole day seems too long, try it with just one person for a limited time—for instance, the caller asking for donations for their charity (and who won't take no for an answer). You can gradually include more people and extend the time frame. How about adopting a positive attitude toward your coworkers for a whole week?

THE POWER OF THE POSITIVE

The Three-Step Emotional Rescue Plan described in this book isn't about having a perfect life or even a completely pain-free life. In the end, life is still life, with all of its challenges, mysteries, comedies, and tragedies. Some days may be stormier than others, but you know that sunshine will follow the blustery weather.

It helps to have a positive outlook when you're trying to see beyond your patterns. It's not just the flip side of a negative or pessimistic attitude. You're not wearing rose-colored glasses—you can see challenges very clearly. But instead of only focusing on how hard it all is, you see possibility and potential within the intense energy of your emotions: anger's brilliant clarity; jealousy's content and generous heart; attachment's pure love and compassion. There's a lot of good stuff there, right within the agitation, doubt, and loss of confidence. You miss a lot if you're looking only at the downside or if you're looking away from the action.

Positivity is more than an attitude or mode of thinking. It's a force that goes beyond words—and you can feel its power in the world at times. When something extremely positive (or negative) occurs somewhere, that place seems to become invested with an energy that can be sensed. It becomes a kind of power spot. Across the planet there are many such spots: sacred mountains, ancient temples, and holy places of pilgrimage that attract visitors hoping for an extraordinary encounter—a magical experience of peace, healing, or awakening.

Every year people throng to these timeless and mystical spots: the ruins of Machu Picchu and Stonehenge, the sacred sites of Jerusalem, the great pyramids of Egypt, and the Bodhi Tree in India, where the Buddha is said to have reached his enlightenment. But I doubt anyone makes these journeys just to see crumbling bricks or an ancient tree. I'm pretty sure the attraction is to the events that unfolded there—the emergence of some transcendent creative energy that still touches the world and moves people's hearts. So the attraction is never just about the physical environment; it's about a felt, inner experience.

Likewise, if in our own lives we can create a degree of positive energy through our intentions and actions, we can have a positive influence as well. If that positivity is strong enough, not only will we benefit, but others will feel it, too. They may sense it as peace or openness or joy. We've heard about these kinds of power spots and their magic, but we may not have realized that we had one right inside of us. All we need is to make this discovery and then we can cultivate it.

Transforming all your negative emotions into a positive

force all at once would be great, but it's unrealistic. If you're pressuring yourself to do too much, then you're going back to your usual habit of torturing yourself. Instead, start with one small thing, one habit, and change that for the better. When you're successful at that, work with the next habit, and the one after that. This way you'll be happier and the work becomes more approachable.

THERE MUST BE JOY

The more positive you can be, the more you'll be able to go about this transformation, this Emotional Rescue project, with a sense of genuine enthusiasm. Really, there must be some kind of joy. You have to see the rewarding part of working with your mind. To explore your mind in a new way, to see it in a different light—wouldn't it be nice? Aren't you tired of your old habits? You're seeing how you can change, how you can transform one habit at a time. If you can generate some kind of enthusiasm, you can enjoy the process. Then it's not a burden. You're not under pressure. *Oh, I must do this, or someone is going to get mad,* or *I'm going to be condemned to hell.* Instead, just take one step at a time and do what you can. Don't overanalyze or overreach. You don't have to accomplish everything at once. When negativity flashes through your mind, flash back with a smile and a kind word. Just try it.

If you can be kind to yourself, whatever your situation,

it can become an opportunity to wake up to your own wisdom and compassion. Eventually you'll reach a stage where everything flows together naturally. As soon as you hear the rumblings of an emotional outburst, you're ready to put into practice everything you've learned: in a flash, you feel the energy, hold it, and look at it directly. Your vision expands until you see the big picture. You get in touch with your senses, body and mind, and then relax and let it all go. You still follow a sequence, but you don't have to stop and think: *What do I do first, then second, then third?* You know what steps to take to turn a bit of insanity into a burst of inspiration.

Your emotional response can become as fluid as the leaps and spins of a dancer. Don't worry if it looks bad to you. And don't be too proud if it looks good. Everything changes and transforms in life, just as it does in your dreams. You could change in the next moment, right? That's the gift of renewal that your emotions offer you. So keep your cool. Be open. Be calm and be honest with yourself. You don't need to present yourself as something or someone else. Just be who you are and click into that—play with and enjoy your dreamlike emotions, but do it mindfully and with your whole heart.

ℒ Now assess . . .
How am I doing?

Once a week, assess. Do you consistently remember your intention as you go about your day? Can you recall the different emotions that come up, and which are most extreme? If you find you're forgetting, losing your focus and resolve, consider reviewing the previous exercises and the goals you set for yourself. The more specific and measurable your objectives, the more likely you are to accomplish them.

Using Distraction as a Helper

In daily life, our surroundings are constantly changing, making it hard to remain present and mindful. Our attention is pushed and pulled by the events going on around us, as well as the constant flow of thoughts and feelings passing through us. That's what we call being *distracted*— our attention is diverted from the here and now—and we usually don't recognize that we've gotten sidetracked until after the fact.

You can turn the tables on distraction and make it your helper, however. You can find ways to apply the Mindful Gap practice anywhere and anytime: waiting for an elevator, in a Starbucks line, during *CSI* commercial breaks, at a red light. You can decide to use just about anything as a reminder to pause and check in with yourself: *Where am I? What am I feeling and doing?* You can set the alarm on your phone to ring or vibrate once or twice a day as a friendly reminder to look at your mind in that moment.

Take Action

In the next week:

- Commit to bringing about a Mindful Gap moment at least once a day.
- Reinforce your intention in the morning as you wake up and in the evening as you go to sleep.
- When you catch yourself getting irritated or annoyed with someone who often challenges your limits, try to use that moment of mindfulness to bring a sense of compassion to the interaction.

EXERCISES AND POINTERS

Notes on Further Training

⟡

In this section, you'll find a number of mindfulness exercises and pointers that will help you succeed in the three steps of the Emotional Rescue Plan. Each exercise will help you strengthen the habit of mindfulness, as well as make your powers of observation more precise and effective.

For any kind of mindfulness training to work for you, you have to be present in your life. That includes being present—mind and body—when your emotions are stirring things up. That's when you want to be clear about your thoughts, and clear about what you see, hear, and feel. That's when mindfulness really becomes your greatest friend. The mindfulness habit is essential to all three methods (Mindful Gap, Clear Seeing, and Letting Go) for working with the emotions. No matter where you are or what you're doing—

you can look at your mind and actions. You can see what's going on around you. You can remind yourself to feel the energy of your emotions and to breathe, relax, and let go.

The first set of exercises, "Mindful Gap: Look," relates mainly to step one. These exercises focus on you and your personal experience of emotions. The second set, "Clear Seeing: Explore," relates mostly to step two. These exercises expand the focus outward to include your relationships and communication choices. The third set, "Letting Go: Relax" relates mainly to step three. These exercises explore your experience of your environment and your sense perceptions, and how you release emotional stress.

While each of the three sets of exercises tends to emphasize one of the three steps in particular, as you do them you may find yourself moving around. You may start out in step one of the ER Plan but move to step two in the course of doing the exercise. Or you might move from step two to three, instead of staying solely with the particular step suggested by the title of that exercise. It will depend on your own experience and perspective—but it's helpful to notice what's happening as you go.

In every exercise, however, you're asked to pay attention, to observe, to see. What are you asked to see? Yourself, your habits, what you're feeling. Taking a close look at these will give you invaluable knowledge you can use to start freeing yourself from the predictable emotional tendencies that bring you misery. Of course, you can keep those that bring you happiness. You'll know the difference.

To start each exercise, read over the commentary and instructions, and then set your intention: *I want to look at my experience of . . . irritation with my kids/dog/partner every morning . . . . I want to observe with mindfulness and see how it changes if I don't react to it.* As you hold your intention firmly in mind, continue with the exercise.

8

Mindful Gap: Look

→ LOOK . . . *Mindfulness at the Kitchen Sink*

CHOOSE ONE OR two ways you can apply mindfulness in your daily life in the coming week. The more specific you are in choosing the activities, the more likely you are to follow through. It's much easier to apply mindfulness to doing the dishes than it is to apply it to something vague, like, "I promise myself to be mindful all day."

You might choose washing the dishes on Monday, Wednesday, and Friday to begin your mindfulness experiment. Simply pay attention to each detail of the task.

❖ Bring your awareness to the present moment, to your body standing at the sink, and the warmth of water on your hands. Notice the texture, shape, and weight of each item as you soap its surfaces, rinse, and place in a rack to dry.

❖ At the end of the week, reflect on how the experience of mindful dishwashing was different from your usual way of washing dishes.

❖ Extend your mindful activity to other areas of the kitchen—the counters and floor—as you're ready.

❖ Alternately, you could choose organizing your desktop at the end of the workday.

Whatever activity you choose, remember that mindfulness is equal parts focus and relaxation—it's not about perfectionism or being intentionally slow and self-conscious. Hopefully, it's enjoyable!

→ LOOK . . . *A Shift in Perception*

When we approach an activity with mindfulness, we're not trying to see in some special way, but it does cause a shift in our perception. When we look at our feelings of anger or envy, they're not our prepackaged versions. We see them freshly, with greater clarity. We start to understand how we see—how we perceive and label—and how that alters our experience.

This clarity leads us to a new understanding of who we think we are. It brings perspective to our relationships and our sense of connectedness to the world. When we genuinely want to explore just how our emotions affect the way our life unfolds, mindfulness carries us a long way.

Look and See

❖ Look at a specific action (something you do by yourself), like cleaning up your desk. Once again, start with yourself. Bring your awareness to the present moment, to your body sitting at your desk, and to the objects on and around your desk. (What are their colors, shapes, and textures?)

❖ Notice your thoughts about the objects and the feelings they provoke, as well as your tendency to drift into thoughts about the past or future.

❖ At the first moment you recognize that you're thinking, acknowledge, *Thinking*, and bring your attention back to your body and the present moment.

❖ Next, briefly shift your attention to the mindful mind itself. Watch the watcher of your actions, then return to simple mindfulness.

❖ Repeat a few times.

❖ Reflect on the experience. Did watching the mindful mind change your experience of the original activity in any way?

→ LOOK . . . *The Flow of Activity*

When you apply mindfulness while you're busy doing things—working at the computer, doing the laundry, washing the car or the dog, you're engaged in "mindful activity." You're being attentive to the flow of activity rather than becoming lost in your thoughts about it. As you move about, you're paying attention with mind and body, with all your senses. You're seeing, hearing, and touching the sights, sounds, and objects around you. When you become distracted, you pause and create a Mindful Gap by releasing any mental chatter or feelings that have come up. Again and again, you let go of your thoughts about what you're doing and get back to doing it.

Letting go of whatever's distracting you means that you let go of more than just chatter. You let go of your perfectionism, your boredom, your envy, your worry, as well. And then you return to your activity with relaxed but focused attention. If you're cooking the evening meal, the point is to simply do it and then let go of it. Let the result be just what it is. If you've given something your full attention and made a good effort, it's generally enough. Don't worry about becoming an expert in all facets of your life. Instead, just try to relax and enjoy what you're doing.

Reflect on It

Choose a simple creative activity that's new to you or at which you're inexperienced. For example, draw a picture, arrange some flowers, write a poem. What's important in this practice is to explore an unfamiliar activity with open- ness, and then let go of the result. When you encounter self- criticism, confusion, or resistance, simply pause and relax. That's being kind to yourself.

Using the continuous writing technique described pre- viously, write for five minutes about your experience (lon- ger if inspired to keep going). Here are some questions you might explore:

- ❖ What feelings did you notice as you engaged in the activity?
- ❖ Were you able to meet resistance with curiosity and kindness? If yes, what was that like? If no, what was the barrier?
- ❖ Were you occasionally able to release distracting thoughts? If so, did that help you to appreciate the pro- cess versus anticipate a result?
- ❖ What is it like to observe the result of your efforts with- out labeling (good, bad, beautiful, ugly)?

→ LOOK . . . *Daily Reminders*

For this exercise, the idea is to find similar intentions in two different activities: an everyday activity, like driving a car, and a more exceptional activity, like working with difficult emotions. When you find a common purpose, the result is that performing the everyday activity can remind you of your intention to deal effectively with your emotions.

Reflect on It

❖ Using the example of driving a car, start by asking yourself, *What's my intention when I get behind the wheel of my car? Why do I do it?* Your answer might be, *I want to be free to go wherever I want to go—and some are places I could never reach just by walking.*

❖ Next, think about how you work with your emotions. Ask yourself, *What's the intention behind my commitment to work with my emotions? Why do I do it?* Your answer might be, *I keep working with my emotions because it's the only way my life will have less suffering. My intention is to be free of emotional suffering.*

❖ Finally, integrate the two, so that the purpose of the one reminds you of the purpose of the other. It might go something like this: *Just as I drive my car to reach the physical places I want to go, I work with my emotions to reach*

*the inner space I long for—freedom from emotion's suffering.
Just so, each time I drive my car, I'll remember my goal of
freedom.*

❖ To help you remember, decide on a specific cue, for
   instance, when you turn the key in the ignition that
   starts up your car and ignites your mindfulness. You
   can also stick a note on your dashboard.

When you work with an exercise like this, take five to
ten minutes at the end of the day to reflect on how this practice was helpful. Also, look at what interfered with your
ability or motivation to apply mindfulness. You might want
to keep a journal or sketchbook by your bed to make a few
unprompted notes or sketches before going to sleep.

→ LOOK . . . *Catch and Release*

I once bought a shirt at the airport because I had been trav-
eling a long time and was in need of a change. I found one
in a nice deep blue color and put it on without looking
closely at it. Then, when I was sitting in the airplane, I saw
it had a fish on it along with a caption down the sleeve:
CATCH AND RELEASE. I felt very good about that. It was like
a message from the universe: somehow, I was wearing instructions for working with the mind in meditation. That
was my teaching for that trip.

You can use that phrase in your practice of meditation,

or contemplation, too. Catch your thoughts and release them. You don't need to bang them on the head and try to kill them before throwing them back. You can just acknowledge each thought and then let it go.

The practice of meditation is basically a process of getting to know yourself. How do you do it? By becoming familiar with your mind. Normally the mind is a whirlwind of thought, and meditation is a practice that calms this down and helps us develop a peaceful state of mind. Not only is our mind busy thinking, we're usually thinking about the past or the future. We're either reliving old dramas or imagining what could happen tomorrow or in ten years and trying to plan for it. We usually aren't experiencing the present moment at all. We can't change the past, and the future is always ahead of us—we never reach it, have you ever noticed? So, as long as this process continues, our mind never comes to rest. The mind can never just settle down and feel at ease.

When we practice meditation over time, we get better at catching our thoughts and emotions, and releasing them. Gradually the mind begins to settle naturally into a resting state. This is great because it allows us to be fully present in our lives. When we aren't being pulled into the past or the future, we can just be right here, where we actually live. To be in the present moment simply means to be awake and aware of yourself and your surroundings. That's the beginning of peace and contentment.

Instruction: Following the Breath

One of the most effective methods of meditation is the practice of following the breath. To begin, you simply sit in a comfortable and upright posture and watch your breath. There's nothing else to do. Your breathing should be natural and relaxed. There's no need to change your normal breathing. Start with bringing your attention to your breath, focusing on the inhalation and exhalation through your nose and mouth. There is a sense that you are actually feeling your breath, feeling its movement.

When you do this, you're not just watching your breath. As you settle into the practice, you actually become the breath. You feel it as you exhale, and you become one with it. Then you feel the breath as you inhale, and you become one with it. You are the breath, and the breath is you.

As you begin to relax, you begin to appreciate nowness, the present moment. Breathing happens only in the present. Breathe out. One moment is gone. Breathe in again. Another moment is here. Appreciating nowness also includes appreciating your world, your existence, your whole environment, being content with your existence.

How to Begin

To begin a session of meditation, first you need a comfortable seat. You can use any cushion firm enough to support an upright posture. You can also sit in a chair. The main point is to have a relaxed but erect posture so that your spine is straight. If you are sitting on a cushion, cross your legs comfortably, and if you are sitting on a chair, place your feet evenly on the floor. You can rest your hands in your lap or on your thighs. Your eyes can be half open, with your gaze directed slightly downward a short distance in front of you. The most important point is that your posture is both upright and relaxed. Once you're sitting comfortably, the main thing is to be fully present—to give your practice your full attention. It's a good idea to start with short sessions (maybe five or ten minutes), and bring an attitude of curiosity about your experiences. Don't worry about whether you're doing it "right" or "wrong"!

Catching Your Thoughts

During meditation the chatterbox of mind will open up, and you'll have lots of thoughts. Some will seem more important than others and evolve into emotions. Some will be related to physical sensations: the pain in your knee or back or neck. And some will strike you as extremely important—things that can't wait. You forgot to respond to a critical email, you need to return a call, or you forgot your mother's birthday. These kinds of thoughts will come, but instead of jumping up from your meditation, all you have to do is recognize them. When a thought tries to distract you, just tell yourself, *I'm having a thought about forgetting Mom's birthday.* You simply catch your thought, acknowledge it, and then let it go. Sitting in meditation, we treat all thoughts equally. We don't give more weight to some thoughts than to others. If we do, we can quickly lose our concentration. Our mind will start to wander away and get caught up in all kinds of imagination.

We might think our meditation should be completely free of thoughts, with our mind totally at peace, but that's more like the end result of our practice than the process. The "practice" of meditation means relating to whatever comes up for us. When a thought comes up, we recognize it, acknowledge it's there, and then we let it go, relax, and breathe. That's "catch and release."

When you meditate, you repeat this catch-and-release process over and over again. Mindfulness, catching your thoughts, strengthens the power of your concentration with repeated practice, just as you strengthen the muscles in your body every time you exercise. Your mind is connected to many different conditions that impact you in various unpredictable ways. Don't expect your meditation to always be the same or match your expectations for progress.

It takes time to bring our mind to a peaceful and clear state. Eventually, however, you will see that your mind stays where you put it. Meditating and developing strength of mind isn't just a nice, wholesome activity. It is actually a big help and support for anything you want to learn or accomplish. As your mind becomes calmer, you experience more of what is happening in each moment. You begin to see that your life—your actual life, right now—is far more interesting than all those thoughts you've been having about it!

9

Clear Seeing: Explore

→ EXPLORE . . . *Your Personal Limits*

CERTAIN ACTIVITIES, like dancing, singing, painting, or writing, encourage us to be present with uncertainty and explore our creative process. If we can stay open and non-judgmental when we're outside our comfort zone, it's possible to see the play of our thoughts and emotions pretty vividly. At times the whirl of thoughts and emotions can distract us from the simple immediacy of our movements (mental and physical), and then we can become discouraged from exploring further. We reach a stopping point, a personal limit.

You might describe a personal limit as an edge or line you can't cross. You've gone as far as you can go emotionally. If you push yourself any further, you'll burst or fizzle out. You feel stuck, resistant, or angry. When you're reflecting on these experiences of frustration and feelings of failure, can you hear what you're saying to yourself? For instance, you might fall into thinking, *I can't* . . . when you meet up with a persistent and unwelcome emotion, especially one that you feel helpless to change. There can be a subtle underlying belief that you're powerless to do anything about it. It's important to notice this sense of limitation because it separates you from your heartfelt aspiration.

Yet as long as you're making an effort to work with your emotions and thoughts, you're being mindful and aware. You're recognizing and transforming old, unhelpful habit patterns. You can use challenging experiences to become familiar with, and go beyond, what you think of as your limitations.

Personal Limits Are Not Permanent Obstacles

Once you're familiar with your personal emotional limits—you know which lines you don't want to cross—you can use your practice of mindfulness to investigate these tendencies. Like all things, these tendencies of yours have causes and other factors that support their continued existence, and it's helpful to be aware of what's propping them up.

Happy and painful mind states don't simply show up out of the blue. They are the result of a particular group of factors, like the ingredients for making a pie. You get a delicious pie or a tough sour one depending on the ingredients you include or don't include in the pie, the excellence of the recipe, the knowledge and skill of the pie maker, and so on. The piece of pie you see before you isn't inevitable. You could have made it with a cheese crust. You could have added some meat and made a savory pie.

In the same way, our good and bad habits depend on so many things in order to work the way they do. Seeing these interdependent connections helps us understand that our personal limits aren't necessarily permanent obstacles. Long before they show up and frustrate us, they can be interrupted at any point in the process, which will change the general outcome. When you get angry at your boss, you don't have to go home and kick the dog. There's room to maneuver and change the dynamic. You can go beyond those supposed limits, after all. The first step is taking a closer look at the experience of limitation itself, along with the conditions that trigger these feelings.

Take Action:

❖ Set an intention to examine your experience of a personal limit and to apply the practice of mindful gap when you feel this experience arising.

❖ Identify at least one specific instance in which you will apply this intention.

❖ Identify what triggers your experience of limit. For instance: Are you overcome with resentment if a colleague at work, who is not your boss, tells you what to do? Do you lose your temper when your partner contradicts what you say, especially when you know you're right?

❖ Resolve to bring your practice of Mindful Gap into situations where your triggers are commonly present. For instance: becoming anxious or hostile while waiting in long lines.

The important point here is to bring mindful attention together with your feelings of limitation—without judgment—and allowing the Mindful Gap practice to lead you.

→ EXPLORE . . . *Your Emotional Habits in Relationships*

The key to working skillfully with emotions in your intimate relationships is to develop mindfulness of your emotional patterns. It's particularly important to see how you handle the many different expressions of desire. Are you aware of how you react when you're feeling jealous or neglected? Do you see how predictable you are when disappointed? Do you become angry or clingy or begin to plot emotional revenge? What helps you to be open? What sparks your sense of generosity or forgiveness?

One of the best things you can do to preserve your relationships is develop a straightforward and honest relationship with your emotions. If you can see how your emotional habits show up from one moment to the next, you have a much better chance of transforming them. Bringing just a moment or two of mindful awareness to a dicey situation can save you from another roller-coaster ride. You don't have to reject these powerful emotions or run screaming away from them. But you do need to stay mindful of them. A strong habit of mindful attention can help you sustain a happy balance in your emotional life. Finding that balance is not only a better way to live; it can be your path to a wiser and more joyful existence.

Reflect on It

❖ Bring to mind an exchange that went badly. Briefly feel the emotion without reacting, thinking, or judging too much.

❖ Then generate a strong sense of kindness and compassion, first for yourself and then for your partner, family member, or friend. Rest with that for a few minutes, and then watch how your view of the situation changes.

❖ What helps you to return to a state of openness after an argument or painful exchange in an intimate relationship?

❖ Choose one insight from these contemplations (e.g., *Not being so hard on myself helps me find my sense of humor*) and try applying it the next time you're caught up in a heated moment.

→ EXPLORE . . . *Compassion in Your Community*

Compassion is marked by a willingness to be present with suffering, along with the strong desire to relieve it. Compassion pulls you close to suffering in order to help transform it. If you keep suffering far away from you, it's hard to contribute much. When you bring compassion into your community life and interactions, you can relate better with the diverse and sometimes conflicting perspectives of others.

Cleaning up a street in our neighborhood, working in our community garden, organizing a car pool, or planning a school party—such shared tasks give us a chance to see how we're connected to each other. They also show us how often small shifts in our intention can change our experience of those relationships. For example, do we become more or less friendly and engaged according to who agrees with us and who disagrees? When we adopt an attitude of openness and acceptance toward others, compassion opens the way to harmony. We all want to be happy at the end of the day—friends and family, competitors and enemies. None of us wants to be afraid, sick, or in pain. As we know from our own experiences, there's never any lack of opportunity to reach out with kindness. Ultimately, compassion welcomes relationships, even inconvenient ones!

Reflect on It

Think about an experience you've had while working in a group setting. Consider the following questions, and make a few notes to remind yourself what the experience was like. If possible, find another person or small group with whom you can explore these questions. Together you're likely to come up with your own questions, too.

❖ How did the experience support or challenge your mindfulness or compassion?

❖ When challenges arose, how did you work with them? Were you able to befriend the challenge? If not, what would help you to meet it with curiosity and kindness next time?

❖ How does your sense of mindfulness change when working in a group versus working alone?

❖ What is different for you when you're performing an activity that is not of your own choosing versus one that is?

→ EXPLORE . . . *How You Speak and Listen to Others*

Communication is more than the words we use to convey information to one another. It has energy that is expressed in our emotions. When we talk with one another, the information we exchange is only one part of the conversation.

Our feelings about the information are another part—our actions really do speak louder than words. So, when we listen with our ears only, and not with our heart, we miss crucial aspects of what is being communicated to us.

The following exercise is meant to heighten the contrast between mindful and unmindful activity. If we can be kind to ourselves when we notice those moments we've been forgetful, they can become helpful reminders. There is always next time. There's always a way forward. In our daily life, if we can begin to see this contrast between our mindful and unmindful activity, as well as the difference it makes to us, we may begin to notice positive changes in our relationships: greater trust, appreciation, and harmony.

TWO-PERSON EXERCISE

In the following exercise, you and a partner will explore the process of speaking and listening, with specific emphasis on **listening**. Each person will take a turn as the speaker and the listener. So each of you will have a chance to experience both roles. The roles are described first, followed by the specific guidelines for the exercise.

Listener

Your practice in this role is to listen fully to your partner while paying attention to your feelings. Notice your reactions to what you're hearing. Often, when we're in conversation with another person, we feel the need to jump in and say something right away. We get caught up in our desire to respond, to answer, or to fix a problem. This desire plugs up our ears and we can no longer hear what our friend is saying.

So just listen and be open. In this openness, if you find yourself getting emotional, simply apply the Mindful Gap practice. This will help you hold still and refrain from any impulse to respond to what your partner is saying. Keep watching the flow of your thoughts and feelings (patiently) without trying to change them. Then, let go and rest in the experience of listening.

This practice can feel awkward and uncomfortable at first. If you feel that way, take it as a good sign that you're actually doing the exercise. As you get used to listening in this way, your presence becomes truly supportive and helpful to others. Gradually, you can build on these listening skills to include mindful responses. The intent of this exercise, however, is to experience listening on its own.

Speaker

Your practice in this role is to bring mindfulness to your speech. Speak with intention and be as clear as possible. When you're uncomfortable or unsure about what to say, allow silence rather than continuing to talk. Pay attention to the thoughts and feelings that arise when you speak without your partner giving verbal feedback. As feelings come up, pause, simply acknowledge them (either aloud or silently), and continue.

Both Speaker and Listener

This exercise will heighten awareness of your habits of communication, which could surprise you. Ordinarily, our habits of speech aren't so obvious to us. When we're talking to a friend, for example, we're usually intent on getting our own point across, and we're less focused on the message our friend is trying to get across to us. As we apply careful attention to listening and speaking, we can see clearly whether we're going beyond "self-interest or self-gratification."

You're now ready to start . . .

THE EXERCISE

Select a partner and arrange a mutually agreeable time to do this practice.

1. Find a place where you can sit across from each other with a comfortable distance between you (about the width of a table).
2. Choose which of you will be the speaker and the listener for the first part of the exercise. You'll reverse roles in the next round.

3. Together, take a few minutes to reflect on kindness and compassion. Establish a mutual intention to rely on these qualities throughout the exercise, for both yourself and your partner.

`4. *Speaker*: Choose a topic that's personal and current, around which you've been experiencing a mild emotional charge. Initially, pick a topic that's workable, rather than a deeply painful one. Keep it on the lighter side. Maybe something happened at work this week, or there's something in the news that captured your attention.

5. *Listener*: Just listen to the speaker. Do not offer feedback. If any emotional disturbance surfaces, practice Mindful Gap: acknowledge the feeling while setting aside the story line, judgment, or other impulse. Try to remain in contact with the direct experience of the feeling. As much as possible, remain attentive and openhearted toward the speaker.

6. The speaker will have four minutes to talk to the listener. (It's helpful to set an alarm or timer.) This is an opportunity for the speaker to just talk. The partner listens but does not speak in response. Be aware of your mental and emotional experience as you speak. Note how the qualities of "speech" extend beyond the words, and remember to practice Mindful Gap in response to the arising of feelings.

7. Reverse the roles for an additional four minutes. The speaker is now the listener, and vice versa.

Reflect on It

Write for ten minutes in response to one or more of the following questions. You can return later to the questions you didn't answer.

❖ Describe the experience of listening without responding. What did you learn?

❖ Describe the experience of speaking without receiving verbal feedback.

❖ Where did you find kindness most accessible? Where was it least available? For instance, explore any feelings of judgment, negativity, or fear.

❖ Describe a sticking point (the point where your judgment or fear was provoked, or where you noticed it was difficult to pay close attention).

❖ What was the most pleasant part of the exercise?

→ EXPLORE . . . *Listening with Your Heart*

Compassion seems to be the gateway to real communication. When your heart is lit up with compassion and you are beyond pure self-interest or self-gratification, your message will usually get through.

When your partner or parents or children are talking to you, if you listen with a conclusion already there, with judgments and concepts already there, then you never hear what they're trying to say to you. That's why we have miscommunications and problems in relationships with our parents, children, and partners the world over. We don't hear each other, we only hear ourselves. No matter what other people are saying, you hear what you want to hear (your own conclusion, your own judgment, your own belief).

If we're willing to be open, to listen without jumping to conclusions or judgments, then our rigid views can soften, and compassion has a chance to influence the situation. We communicate a quality of trustworthiness, which encourages others to trust in themselves. When compassion and wisdom come together like this, it brings heart to your actions and moves your heart to act. Your aspiration to genuinely help others can actually be realized.

So in order to hear the actual message—the essence of the communication—you must listen from your heart the way you listen to music. And when you listen this way, there's an openness that allows for the merging of two minds, or two hearts, into one.

Reflect on It

If you want to apply compassion skillfully, you have to be sensitive to the needs of the situation. To know what that is, you have to let go of your preconceptions. You look and listen with an open mind and heart.

❖ Think of a situation where you felt you were misunderstood and didn't receive the help you needed because you were not heard.

❖ Now think of a situation where you felt you were in need and also clearly heard.

❖ In these two instances, what was different about the listener?

Listening Practices

❖ Commit to listening with your heart intentionally once a day in the coming week. Name a time, place, and person with whom you'll do this practice.

❖ Reflect on the intention of kindness and compassion in your listening practice.

❖ Identify a relationship that is likely to benefit from this kind of practice: your partner, your child, a colleague at work, a member of your social community.

❖ When you next see that person, listen with your heart.

> ❖ *If the relationship is intimate and the person you're talking with is open to it, you might explain that you're learning a practice to cultivate kindness in communication. Maybe they'll be interested in exploring the process with you. If they are, you can explain the practice and try it together: agree on a question and review the speaker's and listener's roles before you begin.*

❖ In public or work-oriented situations, experiment with giving your full attention to conversations at certain times (e.g., during one portion of the day), and then let go of the practice at other times. Notice how these interactions differ.

❖ If no one is available to listen to, turn on the radio and listen to the news. When listening, notice any emotions and apply Mindful Gap.

10

Letting Go: Relax

→ RELAX . . . *Where You Are*

Think Back

REFLECT FOR A moment on an experience you've had of walking into a familiar setting like a lecture hall or conference room (or some group setting). Each time you entered the room, did you already know where you were going to sit? Did you have a favorite spot? What did you notice as you walked in? Was it quiet or chatty? Was there a sense of orderliness or was it messy and chaotic? Did the room's atmosphere affect your own sense of comfort and mood? Did you feel any desire to change the room in some way?

How difficult is it for you to accept the environment you find yourself in, just as it is, and let go of trying to change it? When you're sitting in the dentist's waiting room, do you start wishing it had more comfortable chairs, newer magazines, and a few real windows? It's fine to have preferences (we all do), but at what point does a preference become a rejection of your environment that disturbs your mind?

Think Now

Where are you right now? What do you see? What do you feel? Observe the experience of your senses in relation to the room around you at this moment. Notice physical sensations—the contact between your body and the cushion or chair beneath you, the quality of the air on your skin, the light and images perceived by your eyes, and the ambient sounds. Is there a scent in the air, a lingering taste on your tongue?

When you feel "all here," in touch with your surroundings, let go of the effort that got you here and just relax.

Think Ahead

The next time you find yourself in a group, pay attention to where you're standing or sitting in relation to others. Proximity to or distance from others may generate certain feelings. What does it feel like to be in the middle of a group rubbing elbows with your neighbor as compared to standing by yourself apart from the crowd? Notice your reactions, your preferences, and the labels you attach to the experience: *This is good* or *This is bad*, *I'm comfortable* or *I'm uncomfortable*.

The moment you catch that process of labeling or judgment beginning—pause and briefly apply the practice of Mindful Gap: Feel, Hold, and Look. Step back and look at the big picture. Connect with your body, take a deep breath, let go, and relax. Release whatever you're holding on to, or whatever is holding on to you.

Examining our experience in this way helps us become aware of tendencies that often go unnoticed. It helps us see how things are, in contrast to how we think they are. It also helps us develop sympathy, kindness, and compassion for ourselves, which helps us feel the same for others.

→ RELAX . . . *Connect with Your Senses*

For all the advantages we enjoy as inhabitants of this modern cyber-world, there are some losses as well. Despite our passion for the physical—yoga, athletics, jogging, or sex—we have, to some extent, lost track of our bodies. We sometimes treat them as nothing more than a machine to get us to the latest cool tablet, smartphone, Xbox, or 3-D TV. We routinely replace genuine emotion with intellect—with thinking and talking about our feelings rather than feeling them. Often it takes a calamity like a car crash, or an ulcer, or a hurricane to wake us up to the present experience of our body.

Simple sensory perception exercises are one means of re-claiming the "feeling sense"—our sense of contact with the physical world. What follow are suggestions for a beginning practice to reconnect with the five senses: sight, sound, smell, taste, and touch. These five senses face "outward," toward all the interesting, beautiful, ugly, desirable, and scary things in our world. Yet they have an inner aspect as well. Our senses are seated in our bodies. When outer and inner are con-nected, our experience is more complete and profound. In the beginning, it's helpful to do these exercises by yourself to avoid triggering your habitual responses to other people.*

FRESH SIGHT

1. Find a comfortable, quiet place in your home or in a nat-ural outdoor setting, if possible. Take a seat in an upright, relaxed posture, and let your eyes rest on a natural object like a flower (in a vase is fine), a tree, or a stream. It's best not to focus on man-made items (park benches, bicycles, lampposts) or other people in the beginning. Try to see both the object and its surroundings (the forest and the trees) without focusing too tightly or tiring your eyes.

---

* The exercises on working with the outer and inner senses are adapted from the work of Nalandabodhi Mitra Lee Worley, author of *Coming from Nothing: The Sacred Art of Acting* (Turquoise Dragon Press). Ms. Wor-ley is also a founding member of Naropa University.

2. Let go of expecting anything to "happen" and allow your eyes to simply look. Labels, thoughts, and comments may come into your mind, but just let them pass through.

3. Imagine that you're able to see through all the pores of your body. Let your eyes keep drinking in the sight of the tree (or other object).

4. There might come a point when you think you've completed the experiment. This is the point where you renew your attention, resting on the flower, tree, or stream a little while longer (two or three minutes).

5. As you keep at it, begin to tune in to how your body feels inside and out. Don't put labels on these feelings. (Gently let go of any labels that come up.) Instead, see if you can identify where in your body you are feeling any sensation, even if you think these feelings (a cramp in the leg or stiffness in the neck, for example) have nothing to do with what you're looking at. If a sensation moves or changes, don't try to hold on to it, just notice what it is doing. Continue noticing and feeling what's happening in your body.

6. When you conclude the exercise, rest a moment and take your time getting up and leaving. Notice any thoughts that come up about the exercise—how well or poorly you did it, what it meant, etc.—and simply let go of them. By doing this, you're building up your "letting-go" muscles.

NATURAL SOUND

1. Choose a piece of music you enjoy, starting with music that's not atonal or too wild. Don't listen with headphones.

2. Get comfortable. Imagine that you are able to hear through all the pores of your body. Put your full attention on the sounds as they come into all these "ears." If you catch yourself drifting into fantasies or other thinking, simply return your attention to the sounds.

3. Just as in the exercise with sight, begin to tune in to how your body feels inside and out. Don't put labels on these feelings. (Gently let go of any labels that come up.) Instead, try to identify where in your body you are feeling any sensation, even if you think these feelings (cramp in the leg, stiffness in neck) have nothing to do with what you are listening to. The idea is to keep allowing the sounds to enter your body and to notice where in your body these sounds resonate.

4. Music can be particularly evocative of emotions. If this happens, see if you can locate where in your body the emotion is located. Bring your attention to that spot and relax. Instead of resting in the feeling, however, you may notice that your attention wanders quickly away from the emotion to the story we tell ourselves about the emotion. Such noticing is good, as it reveals our habit of thinking about our feelings rather than feeling them.

When you notice, just gently return to the physical sensations of the body and the pure emotion.

5. To conclude, allow a few deep breaths before getting up and going back to your day.

Bright SMELL

1. Choose an object that has a distinct scent, such as a fragrant flower or a stick of cinnamon or incense, and then sit comfortably. Close your eyes and focus on the scent.

2. As you breathe in, imagine that the scent comes in through your nostrils and fills your body with its perfume. Relax your abdomen and let your breath become peaceful and full.

3. While resting in the awareness of or experience of the scent, again tune in to how your body feels and let go of any tendency to label these feelings. Then begin to investigate which parts of your inner body (or sensations within your body) are awakened or roused by the smells. Imagine your body is hollow like a balloon and receive the scent without blockages. Are there places that are not touched by the scent? If so, mentally connect with these places and encourage them to fill with the perfume.

4. When you begin to get bored, stay with this exercise a little longer.

5. Conclude this exercise by just resting in your body and allowing yourself to breathe naturally.

Variation: When you're ready for a slightly greater challenge, try this: First, allow the scent to ride in on your breath and fill your hollow body completely. Then, as you exhale, watch as it escapes out through your nostrils and all the pores of your body, perfuming the space of the room—or beyond the room, if you like, to your neighborhood, city, country, etc. As far as you want to go.

PURE TASTE

Prepare two bite-sized pieces of a juicy fruit on a plate. Peaches and strawberries are especially fine, but any fruit will do. Begin by just sitting comfortably with the plate in front of you. By now your experience with the previous exercises will guide you as you settle and feel your body.

1. First, investigate to see what feelings or sensations are stirred up by looking at or thinking about eating the fruit. The first piece of fruit will be eaten in stages, much slower than you generally eat.
2. Pick up one piece of fruit and place it on your tongue. Close your mouth and let it rest there. What internal body sensations do you notice?
3. Gently begin chewing the fruit, but do not swallow yet. Feel the juices grow in your mouth and your teeth coming together, squishing the fruit. Taste the fruit.

What is the internal body sensation now, in response to chewing or tasting?

4. Next, swallow the fruit. Notice the inside of your mouth, the motion of your throat, and the feeling of the fruit descending into your stomach. Rest with this experience briefly.

5. Now, turn your attention to the aftereffects of eating the fruit. Where in your body do you notice any physical sensations? Do they last or change?

6. Repeat the sequence with the second piece of fruit. See if you can go through the entire process smoothly (and a little more quickly, if you wish) while maintaining your mindfulness.

Variation: See if you can maintain your mindfulness of any feeling sensations, and at the same time reflect on the story of the fruit, how it grew, was picked, shipped, displayed, purchased, and all the people and other conditions such as sunshine and water that went into the creation of this delicious fruit and your consumption of it in that moment.

Clear Touch

This final sensory exercise explores the sense of touch. By this time you should have an increasing access to your inner sensory world due to your earlier investigations of the other "outer-facing" senses. Although the experience of touch is always with us, touch is the most diffuse of the outer sense perceptions. It can be difficult to pinpoint the actual sensation. Sometimes it's quite simple—like stroking the fur of a kitten. It can also be highly complex—like sensations that evoke the experience of compassion or tell us we're falling in love. When someone does something especially kind, you may say it was "touching" or that you were "touched" by that kindness.

We're investigating our sensory experiences as a warm-up for dealing with our dynamic, sometimes problematic emotions, such as anger, envy, passion, and the rest. The following exercise goes beyond the physical sensation of touch to explore how we allow ourselves to be touched by our world.

1. Choose a photograph of someone you know, for example, a person or a pet.
2. Seat yourself comfortably, and after settling into your body, pick up the photo and look at it for a moment. Then close your eyes. Allow yourself to feel the presence of the person or animal in the photo. Notice any sensations in your body sparked by this first step.
3. After a few minutes, open your eyes and continue to feel the presence (or you could say, vibration) of this person or animal. If you begin to have many thoughts, gently return to simply noticing your sensations of the body and breathe in a relaxed manner.
4. Letting go of any stories about the person or pet, see if

you can widen the circle of your awareness. Expand your attention outward so that you feel the space of the room you're in. At the same time, remain aware of your body and the space between you and the photograph. Stay with this extended awareness for a bit.

5. Once you're able to do the previous step, gently allow some thoughts about the person or pet to arise in your mind. Try not to manipulate or manage these thoughts. Just notice which thoughts come up all by themselves. Stay awake in the space and in your body. If your thoughts start to carry you away from this broader awareness, come back to just your body and personal space. Once again, investigate where in your body you feel "touched" by the presence of the person or pet in the photograph.

6. As you close the session, send thoughts of caring and kindness to this person or animal from the area of your heart. You can imagine these wishes extending out like rays of sunlight. This is an opportunity to wish them the same happiness and freedom from suffering that you wish for yourself.

7. Then rest in these feelings. You don't need to hurry away. You can also send your good wishes out beyond the space of the room to others both familiar and un-known to you.

11

It's Not About Being Perfect

✓ Who Are Your Role Models?

Think of someone you know who inspires you because of their personal qualities of grace, kindness, or intelligence, as well as their actions in service to others. It's helpful to have such role models and mentors. Their example can help us to keep going and overcome our own doubts, fears, and obstacles. They inspire us to believe in ourselves and in our potential.

Such a relationship (even if it's remote, a heartfelt admiration for our favorite teacher or artist) can encourage us to discover within us resources of courage and determination we didn't know we had. We learn to appreciate what it means to take responsibility for our own discomforts and challenges. We learn to care for ourselves. By making friends with our own life and gradually opening up to our emotions, we begin to let go of the impulse to lay blame. We feel more comfortable in our own skin and more willing to share our experience with others. Kindness becomes a part of our day-to-day existence and compassion develops naturally. As we become braver, our example encourages others to be more daring as well.

Reflect on It

❖ Do you have a role model—or several?

❖ What qualities do you most admire in your role model?

❖ In what way do those qualities exemplify kindness or bravery?

❖ How have you been influenced or guided in your actions by his or her example?

❖ Are you a role model for anyone?

✓ REVIEW YOUR GOALS AND INTENTIONS

Once a week, ask yourself questions that will help you assess your progress and renew and invigorate you intentions. You can use these questions, and you can also come up with your own. Make weekly notes in your journal or notebook and occasionally review past entries.

❖ How often do I remember to be mindful of my habitual patterns and work with my emotions? Am I remembering more often each week?

❖ What emotions came up for me this week and which were most extreme?

❖ What steps of the Three-Step ER Plan did I use this week? Which were most helpful with my extreme emotions?

❖ What is it about my emotional life that I most want to change? Why is that change so important to me—what would be different in my life if I could make that change?

❖ Are the techniques of Mindful Gap, Clear Seeing, and Letting Go doing what I expected? If not, in what way is my experience different from those expectations?

❖ Am I learning to be kind to myself? Can I remember any times during the week that I stopped an outpouring of criticism and turned it into encouragement or praise?

❖ What do I wish for myself? For others in my life?

Be as specific as you can. If you find you're losing your focus and resolve during the week, review one or two of the previous exercises and reset a positive goal for yourself. Decide to accomplish something reachable in the coming week, as well as affirming your longer-term goal of freeing yourself from your negative emotions.

✓ IF YOU'RE MAKING AN EFFORT, YOU'RE MAKING PROGRESS

Mindfulness, as the name suggests, is essentially a process of working with your mind. It's helpful to remember, however, that the process is a mixed bag, particularly in challenging times. On one hand, there's a sense of transformation taking place: in some areas you'll be overcoming obstacles and experiencing some level of emotional freedom. In other areas, however, you're still struggling, still engaged in negative, unproductive actions, and experiencing the negative results of that. No one is always perfect, and our life includes blunders and burdens of various kinds.

When you realize that you've made a few mistakes or you're caught up in a fit of emotion or fear, you're likely to feel that you've failed. But don't lose sight of the big picture. You don't have to take that to mean that you're not progressing on your chosen path or being successful in life. As long as you're working with your mind, in whatever way you can, you're making progress. (Wasn't there a time when you weren't doing that?) As long as you're making an effort to recognize old patterns and work with them, you're undermining their power. You're cultivating a more positive ground for a happier future. From this perspective, failure is part of what makes up our accomplishments. We often don't see that.

Success in working with your emotions, as in life, isn't

about being perfect. You can't expect that each time a tur-
bulent state of mind knocks on your door, the "normal"
thing is to immediately recognize its true nature. You can't
say it won't be possible at some point, but it's not the "norm."
In the same way, if you expect that each year your income
will increase and your business will grow, that your next
home will be larger than your last, and that you are building
toward a more and more secure and comfortable future, as
befits the American Dream, you are mistaking that ideal for
what's normal. That's not only a mistake, it sounds somewhat boring, like a formulaic movie where you know from
the beginning exactly what's going to happen. In actual life,
anything can and does happen. That is the truth of imper-
manence and change, and it is what makes our life such an
adventure. Remembering this and taking it to heart allows
us to be more pragmatic and, at the same time, more courageous.

We need warriorlike courage to be able to face and accept defeat now and then, and to transform our suffering
and confusion into a more mindful and awake existence.
Like champions in boxing or the martial arts, we have to
accept some defeats and be willing to learn from them in
order to be victorious in the end. Sometimes it feels like the
world sees us as a punching bag, and we're taking hits from
all sides. That's when we need to remember that loss, disappointment, sadness, and pain are part of our life and the lives
of everyone. As your confidence grows and you become
more skillful at working with your mind, you can move

away from chasing after an impossible ideal. You can connect with your life as a personal journey, one that is full of surprises and fresh opportunities to make it meaningful. How it goes and what it looks like is up to you. But if you really want to help yourself and the suffering world, let your compassion blaze.

PART TWO

Exploring Emotions Further:

A Classic Buddhist

Approach

12

The Way of the Buddha

*There is only one corner of the universe
you can be certain of improving,
and that's your own self.*

—ALDOUS HUXLEY

WHEN I BEGAN to share my experience of working with emotions with my friends in the West, I realized I needed to understand the emotions from a Western point of view in order to communicate from a sense of common ground. Otherwise I would just be furthering the general confusion. So I approached a number of friends—psychologists, psychotherapists, and psychiatrists—and asked them how "emotion" is defined in their fields. What I learned is that there is no single definition of emotion among these professions. There are many different working definitions, depending on one's training and objectives. Then there are the explanations we all have for the emotions that regularly end up in our dreams, our songs, and our stories. So there's still a lot of work to do before we truly understand the relationship between our mind and brain, or first-person experience, and what scientists are able to observe.

At this point, I'd like to explain the origin of the teachings on the wisdom of emotions and the Emotional Rescue Plan from the perspective of classic Buddhist thought. The Buddhist tradition includes extensive studies of the mind based on thousands of years of philosophical investigation, contemplation, and meditative experience. The essence of this wisdom has been passed down from experienced teachers to avid students in an unbroken line all the way from the time of the Buddha, ensuring that these teachings would remain authentic and fresh. Throughout the ages, the first step on the way to understanding your emotions has been to get to know your mind. This means getting to know the busy swirl of thoughts and feelings, hopes and fears, that is driven to joy and tears by the "me" that's you.

THE WISDOM OF EMOTIONS

The teachings of the Buddha are commonly presented in three stages, or progressive levels of instruction. Each stage develops an aspect of the full realization of our potential as human beings, and each stage has its own approach to getting us across its particular goal line. These stages correspond to the three ways of looking at our emotions in the Emotional Rescue Plan: as negative, positive, and neither, or unbiased.

The initial stage of the journey is where we focus on ourselves and our personal freedom. By facing our internal conflicts, we learn to be strong, independent, and responsible for our own emotions. This is where we learn what our problems are and what's needed to overcome them. We develop a strong resolve to at last free ourselves from our suffering. Once we've developed a certain power and confidence in working with our own mind and emotions, in the second stage we can begin to extend ourselves to others. Our world becomes bigger and more inclined to relationship. Finally, in the third stage, our awareness opens out, naturally connecting with the vivid energies all around us.

So how do we work with our emotions according to this three-tiered system? In Buddhist literature, there are three primary emotions: passion, aggression, and ignorance. All other disturbing emotions evolve from these three and contain elements of them. We work in stages to transform all of these negative energies and return them to their natural state of clear, sympathetic awareness. One helpful practice is to examine your experience each day and try to recognize when any of the three primary emotions surfaced and acknowledge the trouble they caused.

Shantideva, a great Indian master of the eighth century, gave this example for how obsession—a close relative of passion—can cause pleasure to cross over into great suffering: Imagine you find some honey. It smells so sweet you have a strong desire to taste it. But there's a problem: This tasty honey isn't in a nice bowl with a spoon. It's coating a very sharp razor blade. So you lick at the honey lightly. But it's so delicious you want a little more. You lick it again a little harder, and then again, a little more enthusiastically still, until your craving for the honey takes you over. The more obsessed you become, the harder and harder you lick the honey. Although your first taste brings a sense of delight, once your desire for it is inflamed, you don't realize that with each lick, you're cutting off part of your tongue on the razor underneath. This example is rated R for violence.

Somewhat different kinds of suffering are caused by the emotions of aggression and ignorance. When your mind is controlled by anger, it's impossible to find any sense of peace. Your body vibrates, your mind seethes. You can't concentrate or relax or even get a good night's sleep. And when you're operating under the influence of ignorance, you suffer from a kind of blindness. Like trying to make out objects in a dimly lit room, your perceptions are vague. You don't see your emotions when they come up or understand their effects or the actions they lead you to. Essentially, you don't recognize the connection between your suffering and the ignorant mind. There's a quality of ignorance, or limited understanding, within all the disturbing emotions. That unawareness transforms into lucid awareness and insight through the practice of the Buddhist path.

So long as we don't understand how our emotions work, we're at their mercy. We can be happy one moment and feel sad and alone the next. There's no weather channel for our emotions. We don't know whether to expect sunshine or clouds each day. Why can't we just be happy? The Buddha said that the cause is our clinging to a mistaken notion of the self. This self, the "I" or "me" that's the center of our personal universe, is not quite all it seems. We tend to attribute qualities to it that it doesn't actually possess.

For example, we feel that this "I" is fundamentally the same from moment to moment, day to day, year to year. "From birth until this very moment, I have been me. While there are certain kinds of changes (growth and aging of body, intellectual development, accumulation of memories and experiences), there's something I recognize as 'me' that is beyond those kinds of changes." What that could be remains vague, but it's the notion of a fixed, enduring self that we cling to, despite all evidence to the contrary.

Looking for this self, or personal ego, is a central practice of the Buddhist path. No matter where we look for it (in the body, the mind, up in the sky), it cannot be found. What we do find is a beautiful, rich, creative, dynamic flow of experiences. We find the world of the senses and a stream of thoughts, feelings, and imaginations. On some instinctive level, we sense that what we're clinging to is only an illusion of permanence and solidity. Do we let go or hang on? Do we lean in to a new experience or follow the ego's command to stand our ground and fight? From this tentative space of doubt and grasping come the disturbing emotions to distract us from the direct experience of our true self. We find ourselves standing alone on a battleground of conflicting feelings and ideas, choicelessly transformed into a warrior.

13

The Warrior
on the Battlefield

Love is the only force capable of
transforming an enemy into a friend.

—MARTIN LUTHER KING, JR.

IN THE FIRST stage of working with the emotions, we come to see disturbing emotions as the enemy and ourselves as a warrior on a battlefield. Ordinarily when we say "enemy," we're referring to someone who causes us harm, inflicting pain and suffering on us. In this sense, the negative emotions that have hurt us so deeply and for so long are true and worthy enemies.

EMOTIONS AS THE ENEMY

To see yourself as a warrior on a battlefield is a traditional example from the Buddhist sutras. On this battlefield, you are fighting one-on-one, face-to-face with your enemy. You have to deal with each challenger forcefully and without hesitation or you are lost. Aggression, passion, jealousy, arrogance, ignorance, anxiety—all have their ways of destroying your sense of well-being and happiness. So when you're facing a powerful emotion that's threatening your sanity, what do you do? At the very moment the emotion attacks, you try to destroy it. You try to defeat these negative energies before they can overpower you. How well you fight and how skilled you are with your weapons depends on how well you've accomplished your basic training (in the arts of study, contemplation, and meditation).

As you gain experience on the battlefield, you develop a warrior's wisdom. You come to possess an in-depth knowledge of your enemies' strengths and weaknesses—especially their strengths. So you never underestimate your enemy. You also possess self-knowledge. You know your own strengths and weaknesses in battle and you know when you need to seek further training. Armed with these two kinds of wisdom, you're prepared to outsmart your enemies. When an emotion rises up against you, you recognize its destructive power. You know what you're dealing with. You remember how even an innocent-looking thought of aggression can suddenly blow up and cause terrible suffering if you lose your mindfulness and awareness.

In the war taking place on the battlefield of your mind, you have the enemy, the Emotional Mind, and the ruling king of that mind, the Ego, fortified by all your ego-clinging. Then you have the generals of the king—the three poisons of Passion, Aggression, and Ignorance. And there you are on the front line of the battlefield with hordes of enemies approaching. They're armed with the latest high-tech weapons of Ego. Behind them are teams of engineers dedicated to keeping the troops on their feet and advancing toward you. At this point, you have to admit you're alone on this battlefield, but you are standing there full of courage and strength.

At the same time, you know you have certain weaknesses. You're not going to win every battle. If the enemy force is too strong, if you can't defeat the generals and their armies of negative mind, then you might as well run. Sometimes the wisest move you can make is a strategic retreat. You shouldn't be a stupid warrior. This is not a suicidal battle.

Where do you go when you run from the battlefield? You run to your meditation cushion. There's nowhere else to go. When you need to learn more about ego and its forces, you run back to your cushion to learn more about how your mind works. You look within to discover the weapons these negative emotions have and the sneaky techniques they're using to overpower you.

At this stage, you approach your emotions with a sense of caution. If you're going to neutralize your mind's negative energy, you have to get to know its negative power very well. So you send out your spies (of mindfulness and awareness) to study their movements and take pictures of their camp until you're really ready to venture out again and test your skills. You can always run away, come back to strike, then run away again. As a clever warrior, you have your own tricks.

There are also those martial arts movies about the underdog kid who gets viciously beaten by the arrogant bully. The boy, wounded and half dead, has no choice but to run away while he still can. He's saved by an old martial arts wizard who trains the boy and turns him into a champion. We see him working with sticks and running and flipping in the air like a monkey. Finally, he learns all the tricks of the warrior. When he faces the bully again, it's a real test of skills. This time, he succeeds in battle, but not through sheer force alone. Through the power of his courage, resilience, and compassion, he cuts through all destructive, negative impulses inside and out, and his enemy, transformed, bows in respect to the boy.

So your meditation cushion is where you discover the inner resources and power to defeat your enemy. There you are finally able to claim the wisdom and compassion that are undefeatable and are naturally yours. When you confidently connect to your own wisdom and compassion, you're ready to go back and meet your enemy, the negative mind. Conquering your own negative mind is actually the same as conquering the negative, emotional mind of others. How is that possible? When you're victorious over your own destructive emotions, you can have a strong impact on your world and bring others to the same level of peace and calmness. We've all heard of people who have done just that—Dr. Martin Luther King, Jr., Nelson Mandela, and Aung San Suu Kyi.

So whenever you need to revive and strengthen yourself, take advantage of the strategic retreat. Then go back again to fight. Warriors never run away forever.

EMOTIONS AS FRIENDS

In the second stage, the warrior takes a different approach to the enemy. You aren't seeing your emotions as simply negative, as something to be rejected or discarded while you go searching for something nicer. Now you see there's a positive side to your emotions. You recognize that by working with the energy of negative emotions you can transform them. Instead of seeing passion, aggression, and ignorance as purely toxic, you know you can use these energies to free yourself from all this emotional chaos.

After so many battles, your old foes are starting to look like friends. You see that if you had no enemies to face, you could never become a warrior. If there were no enemy lands, there would be nothing to conquer. So now when your emotions begin to rise up on the battlefield of your mind, you don't get frightened or irritated. Your bravery arises at the same time. You tell yourself, *I'll let them come!* In fact, you feel happy about it. You see these powerful emotions as being very kind. The challenges they bring will make you stronger!

At this point, your relationship to your emotions has flipped. The impulse is to move closer to them—not to strike a deadly blow, but to make a genuine connection.

You're drawn to your passion and aggression the way you're drawn to people you want to become friends with. Developing this connection between warrior and enemy is a little risky. It requires all of the wisdom and skill at the warrior's command. There's no guaranteed outcome—we're dealing with very strong emotions that may still act like enemies for a while. But as we develop a friendship with them, the power of our enemy becomes integrated into our power. We begin to benefit from the same energy we once fought so hard against.

The goal of a good warrior is to conquer—not kill—the enemy forces and to bring happiness and joy to all sides, to your troops, to your people, and to the people of the enemy. Destruction is *not* the goal. The goal is to transform every kind of suffering into happiness for every kind of being that is capable of feeling and thought. This means your ability to accomplish what your heart desires really depends on how well you're able to connect with your enemy and develop a friendship. This coming-together enriches and heightens all of the warrior's qualities and skills.

EMOTIONS AS ENLIGHTENED WISDOM

In the third stage of working with our emotions, the warrior sees that the emotions' raw power and creativity are themselves the very wisdom of enlightenment. At this point, we take the emotions themselves as the path. We use them to realize the natural wisdom of our mind. We recognize that all those disturbing states—the anger, jealousy, passion, fear, doubt, and anxiety we once ran away from and then tried to transform—are actually expressing different qualities of wisdom. We don't need to stop them or change them. If we can detach our emotional mind from the concepts obscuring it (like clouds that block the light of the sun), then we can actually see the enlightened state of our mind.

Whether you're looking at anger, passion, ignorance, ego itself, or any element of the emotional mind, your emotions are giving you a deeper message than just the pain and discomfort of their disturbing energy. Their vivid presence works like a mirror that helps you see your own face. But you're not standing in front of the mirror in a darkened room. Your awareness is the light that illuminates the space and allows you to see that face reflected in the mirror. Your emotions are helping you see your own true nature (your transcendent self, beyond ego). When you experience that simply, without adding a lot of commentary, there's a sense of oneness or wholeness. At that point, not only will you see your own face, you will recognize it.

The experience of the third stage is difficult to describe because the essential aspects of this transformational process are beyond concept. At this point, the warrior on the battlefield enters a cosmic dimension, and moves according to the intuitive understanding of the heart. The battle with Ego and the generals is still on display but the outcome is no longer in question. The warrior has taken total command

over the great expanse—the vast brilliant space of awareness. He has absolute confidence that the space belongs to
him. It is no longer enemy territory. He has become one
with this great expanse. When the warrior moves, it feels
like all of space is moving, like the whole world is shaking.
Within this unity of warrior and space, your enemies—your
disturbing emotions and ego-clinging thoughts—appear in
the cosmic mirror of space. These colorful images enliven
and ornament the mirror. Without them, the mirror would
be a boring sight.

At this stage, it's as if the warrior rules not only the expanse of space, but also all of the earth and the oceans. The
appearances of passion, anger, and jealousy are like waves in
the ocean. They arise from the ocean of your mind and dissolve back into it. As the warrior sails across the vast ocean
of mind, waves of all dimensions rise up, challenging his
courage and confidence and at the same time beautifying
the ocean. The waves make the journey a bit scary, but also
more interesting and fun. An ocean without waves is pretty
dull. No one wants to navigate that kind of ocean. In the
same way, a mind without concepts and emotions is pretty
dull and stupid.

An ocean beautified by waves is like the warrior who is
ornamented by the appearances of the enemy. What does
this mean? Appearances "ornamenting" your experience
means they make it rich and vivid, even joyful. The warrior
doesn't see the enemy as an enemy anymore—or even treat

the enemy as a friend. The notions of "enemies" and "friends" are at last transcended and become part of your courageous heart. In this moment, victory is spontaneous. Victory is all-pervasive. Victory is this blissful union. The warrior, this heroic being, arises in splendor, decorated with the brilliant ornaments of the enemy.

All of this may be a little difficult to make sense of right now. But that is understandable and fine. This is a journey that takes us to new places. Or perhaps we're returning to a place we've visited before. We've tasted the food and seen a few sites, but now we're ready to learn the language of a country that's starting to feel like home. There's no rush. Day by day we become more familiar with this fresh new environment.

This sense of closeness or unity between the warrior, the space, and the enemy is terrible news for our ego. At the same time, it is great news, because the wisdom we finally find is the wisdom within our ego. The actual one taking this spiritual journey is the ego, after all. The spiritual trip starts out as an ego trip. It's this "bold ego" that wants to set out on a quest to free itself from itself. Ego is searching for the path of egolessness. So there's a kind of magic within this ego-clinging. There's wisdom there.

The same wisdom is present in the ego's generals—our passion, aggression, and ignorance—as well as in the hearts of all those foot soldiers. But we don't see that magic as long as we're looking somewhere else for answers. And we can find answers everywhere, even to questions we haven't asked yet. They're as close as the nearest smartphone. And the genuine wisdom that can transform our lives is even closer than that. We find it by trusting, not something outside us, but our own emotions and their wisdom, and bold beautiful ego, and the wisdom within that ego.

14

What Is a Buddhist?

*Very often a change of self is needed more
than a change of scene.*

—A. C. BENSON

YOU DON'T HAVE to be Buddhist or even spiritually inclined
to use the Emotional Rescue Plan. These methods won't
make you into a Buddhist. But how is this possible, if the
principles and practicalities are rooted in the Buddhist tradition? Maybe it's best to start by looking at the tradition itself.
What is a Buddhist and what is this thing called "the Buddhist path"?

To be a Buddhist means you are willing to actually
work with your mind to develop your inherent potential to
manifest wisdom and compassion. That's the main point of
Buddhism and the defining attribute of a Buddhist. Even
though Buddhism is considered a major world religion, the
teachings of the Buddha aren't necessarily religious, and becoming a Buddhist isn't like joining a church or religious
group. Of course, there is the option of a more faith-based,

religious approach to Buddhism, and there are many examples of that around the world. But to really follow the example of the Buddha himself means something more. It means that you are looking at a much deeper level of your whole being and working to uncover that.

This view of Buddhism is closer to a philosophy of life on the one hand, and a science of mind on the other, in the sense that it's a way of pursuing knowledge of the mind and then using that wisdom to empower our lives. Buddhism practiced in this way is straightforward and down-to-earth.

It can be a way of simplifying things in our lives rather than complicating them, as religion sometimes does. Our lives and our world are already so full of complications. Do we really need another one?

Ultimately, the Buddhist path is about who we are and how we work with our mind, our emotions, and our basic potential. The path is not something "out there" that we need to go out and find before we can work with it. It's not a long climb to some mystical mountaintop. It's not about getting away from our ordinary life at all. The path is about dealing with who we are, what we are, and how we can cut through old negative habits to let our most positive qualities shine.

A key point here is to not separate your life and your path. They may feel separate in the beginning, but bringing these two together makes a huge difference in your experience of the journey. At first you may think, *Okay, this is me, this is my life, and then there's this thing called "my path" that winds in and out of my life.* When we do this, we're treating the path as something special, outside the dailiness of our life, like going to a party. *Okay, now I'm going to my room to meditate.* And then as soon as we leave the room, it's "me and my life" again, and "my path" is nowhere to be seen. If that continues to be our situation, then we haven't really understood the Buddha's teaching.

The Buddhist path teaches a variety of methods for developing the self-knowledge that will free us from even our deepest sufferings. What cause all this suffering are the many layers of confusion that keep us from seeing the clear nature of our minds. Only this confusion stands in the way of us expressing our inherent loving-kindness and compassion.

BUDDHA'S WORKSHOP: SHARPENING YOUR MIND

It is said that the Buddha taught eighty-four thousand methods for working with the mind—leaving us with a kind of something-for-everybody toolbox. In a toolbox of this size, you can find all sorts of devices to use in different situations. If you have a loose screw, do you need a flathead or a Phillips screwdriver to secure it? If you use the wrong tool, you won't get the job done and might make the situation worse. You might destroy the screw, or screw up the hole in your wall. If you use the right tool, it's a very simple job. But tools don't jump out of the toolbox and go to work on their own, yet, do they? No, you have to do the work yourself.

All the instructions of the Buddha for working with our minds are simply tools we can use to fix certain kinds of problems. But first we have to acquire these tools, get to know what each one is for, and then learn how to use them. Not only that, but we have to be willing to use the right tool when the time comes—when things start to fall apart and we're feeling a little shaky.

In this way, the Buddha's teachings are like a self-help project, kind of like what's in the magazines in your doctor's waiting room. As we work with these instructions, we gradually understand what our mind and emotions really are, and we begin to absorb that knowledge until it becomes our personal experience. Finally, that experience becomes so familiar that it deepens into a realization that goes beyond words. It's like reading a book and understanding the words, then experiencing what those words mean, and then actually embodying that meaning by living an enriched and empowered life.

Understanding is developed at first by listening to teachings and attending classes that involve reading and discussing texts. This leads to a clear conceptual understanding of the Buddha's teachings on the mind, and you see that this conceptual mind itself has a bright, lucid quality—it's not just a collection of random thoughts. When we take time to reflect on the understanding we've gained through our learning, experience arises. We don't just keep *thinking* about the mind, we actually *use* our knowledge. We have studied how anger works, so now we can take what we've learned and bring it into an actual experience of our own anger. We let our knowledge and our experience rub together until they create a spark of insight.

At that point, it's a good time to meditate. Meditation is the perfect environment for genuine realization to arise. Realization dawns when that spark of insight blazes up and all confused thoughts are consumed in a fire of wisdom. You can have many sparks here and there over time. They come and go, but once that fire blazes up, your realization of the wisdom of your emotions remains, unchanging.

The practice of meditation we're talking about here is sitting or resting meditation. There are many types of meditation that are taught, some involving the chanting of mantras or the visualization of Buddha images. But the Buddha's instructions for resting meditation are simply to sit. Other than maintaining a relaxed upright posture with a soft gaze and following your breath, there is nothing else to do. When thoughts come, you let go of them.

MORE ON MEDITATION

We're used to constantly thinking about what happened yesterday or might happen in ten years. We're mental time travelers, constantly moving between the past and the future. We're not comfortable just hanging out in the present moment. We'd rather stay busy *doing* something—mentally if not physically. So in the beginning this practice of just sitting sounds pretty radical. But it's proven to be the best way to let go of our usual stress and anxiety, to ease that restlessness that never seems to go completely away.

The point of meditation practice is, first, to change your ordinary habits of being so busy all the time, constantly doing and doing. You can just sit and do nothing for a while. All you need to do is look at your mind. When you do that with mindfulness, remembering to come back every time you drift away, there's not a lot of room for those old habits to do much except make brief appearances. That's a big change.

As you settle into your sitting practice, you come to experience a sense of openness and spaciousness, a clarity and brilliance you recognize as your natural state, the very nature of your own mind. Suffering has no power here—it dissolves as soon as it arises, it vanishes without a trace.

There are many varieties of meditation, but all methods include a sense of settling the mind and body and bringing your awareness to the present moment. You might rest your mind lightly on a visual object or gently place your attention on the coming and going of your breath to help the process of settling. When you take time to sit quietly and meditate in this way, you can relax all that extra effort and simply be who you are. It's a way of getting to know yourself on a much more intimate level. You are just sitting and watching your mind, the coming and going of thoughts, emotions, and sensations—seeing all those and letting them go. You don't have to do anything with them—fix them up, solve their questions, evaluate them, label them, lock them up, or praise or punish them. It's a light, touch-and-go process. The less you bother your thoughts, the less they will bother you.

Eventually, you get to know your own mind. You see what sets it off and what calms it down. You listen while it goes on and on until gradually you become friends. You start to discover not only your mind's tendency to stick stubbornly to its ways, but also its capacity for insight, creativity, and compassion. This busy, often stressed mind we take for granted has so many rich and powerful qualities we never recognized or imagined before.

When you look inward like this, you're entering the creative, energetic domain of the emotions. Soon you can quickly distinguish one emotion from another as they pop into your mind. It's not just one big blur. And all of this comes from simply sitting and watching what happens in your mind, like watching children playing or clouds floating by.

When you've heard a little of the Buddha's teachings on mind and contemplated their meaning, you've opened the toolbox and started learning how to use the tools. With a little meditation practice, you realize you can actually work with your mind—calm it down or wake it up or cool it out. You begin to realize you're in charge and that the path you're on is genuine. Something is clicking. Exploring your emotions is getting even more interesting.

My Mother's Story

My mother told me this story. The first time she went to see a movie in India, she was with a girlfriend. They were watching this movie starring a popular Indian actor. In the movie the actor, a good guy, is being tortured by the bad guys. They beat him up until he's bleeding and has cuts all over his body. Then the bad guys in the movie decide to torture him some more by rubbing salt into the good guy's wounds. My mother said her friend was so upset by this that she stood up and yelled, "No, no, no, stop! Don't, don't do that!" She was screaming out loud in the theater! It's so easy to get lost in another reality. In the beginning, we know we're going to watch a movie—it's just pretend. But after a while we start believing what we see on the screen. In fact, that's what we call a good movie. We get involved in the action and forget we've bought into the moviemaker's illusion. Now it's our illusion, too. We get caught up in the drama of our emotions and end up screaming at lights on the screen.

The question is, how do we work with that? How can we stop spinning this web that we're always getting caught in? We need an exit strategy. So what is our plan of escape?

Meditation is the first place where we meet our mind directly, where we can transform the habitual tendencies that cause us to suffer. We can't change these deep imprints in one face-to-face meeting, but meditation ignites the process of change. We simply bring our everyday life experience of thought and emotion, of our ups and downs, of being stuck and confused—whatever we're going through—to the experience of meditation. Otherwise it's going to be very difficult to figure out what will work best to transform an emotional habit as it starts to take hold. *Uh-oh. Here comes my ex with her new friend.* Whatever mindfulness and awareness we have cultivated in meditation will be key to developing the power to transform a negative tendency on the spot. With time and practice, the process becomes effortless. You won't need to think too much about it.

AT THE END OF THE DAY

At the end of the day, there's no benefit to all our study and contemplation if we're not using it to work with our mind. If all we've done is read some books and think about the words on all those pages, it's like going to a nice restaurant and ordering a fabulous meal, but never getting to the point of actually eating it. Our hunger is never satisfied. In the same way, without practicing meditation, you never get to the point of actually savoring the nature of your own mind. You never get to the place of appreciating and enjoying the wisdom that's the true nature of your emotions. In that case, all that knowledge is like bad money. You can't spend it. You can't use it to get what you need.

There are times of greater and lesser need, of course. When you're happy and healthy with a few dollars to spare, maybe you're not too worried. But when you're struggling with fear and anger day to day, or devastated by a great loss, it's a different story. And a time of great need for all of us is when we're on our deathbed, staring at that white ceiling. Who's going to be there for you when all your attachments, all your regrets and fears, come knocking?

If you're fortunate, you have the support of a loving family and good friends. But your best, most reliable friend at that time is your mind. Beyond a certain point, no one else can take that journey with you. No one else can see what you see or feel what you feel as you move through the transition that marks this life's end. At that moment and beyond, it's just you and your mind. The more you learn about your mind, the more you know what helps it to settle and relax. That's why looking at your mind through meditation is so important. Your last thought might be the one that sets you free.

If you're really familiar with working with your mind, that's all you need. You don't need someone else to save you. You have the tools—the wisdom and power—to completely transform whatever emotions show up to challenge you.

15

Pandora's Box

Heart is what drives us and determines our fate.

—ISABEL ALLENDE

WHEN WE BEGIN to work with our emotions, we have to shine a light into places we've never looked before. It can be a little scary, like opening Pandora's box. We're not sure what we'll find inside. Will we be unleashing dark forces we can't control or stuff back in? Will we discover some kind of fabulous treasure?

When we finally open this box called *the mind*, we find all kinds of things. There are so many thoughts, perceptions, memories, judgments, attitudes, labels, and concepts—fresh and old, active and passive—rumbling around in there. For some, this might be like your kitchen junk drawer. For others, everything's in its assigned place—they've been to the Container Store and have organizers for all their cabinets. Either way, we keep adding to this collection by processing all our experiences through a filter of preconceived ideas and judgments. We're more or less continuously trying to figure out our moment-to-moment experiences, interpreting them through the lenses of Facebook shares, blog posts, and tweets.

On the other hand, there's also a quality of experience that's immediate and direct. It's a kind of close encounter with our world. It's unfiltered. There's nothing between you and that text message, between you and the voice of your child. There's no concept of "good" or "bad" crowding out the vividness of your present experience. There's a moment of simple direct perception followed quickly by a thought. For example, your eye sees an object and then your mind says *flower* or *bicycle*. But just before that thought, there's a sense of original experience that has a quality of genuine human connection. We call this original experience of mind "primordial," which sounds very far away, somewhere in the distant past when dinosaurs walked the earth. But that's not what it means here. Here it means "right now, in this very moment." There's a sense of firsthand experience that's not based on someone else's opinion or perception, or on the perception or opinion of our own thoughts.

All these thought processes, labels, and concepts that come after this have a way of confining or squeezing our experience into a very narrow tunnel. Then you only have tunnel vision. You only see what your thoughts want you to see. You only hear what your thoughts want you to hear. You only smell what your thoughts want you to smell, and so on. That's exactly the opposite of what the Buddha taught about how to work with our mind: When you see a flower, just see it. Simple. Don't add anything. And when you hear a song, just hear it, and so on.

In our everyday life we usually miss this fresh kind of experience. We tend to skip over that moment and wake up when the next set of experiences kicks in. We're right there for our hopes and fears and opinions, but we're somewhere else, lost in thought, when that first pure, direct connection happens.

Why is this important? Direct perception gives us more precise and accurate information, the kind of knowledge we need to follow our rescue plan. It's also more refreshing and energizing to see the true colors of the sky or the shirt you're putting on before going out the door to work.

HOW BUDDHA SEES THE EMOTIONS

According to the Buddha, our emotions are playing within a great field of energy, an expanse of vividness, beautifully bright and full of sparks. And that energy field is like pure water that has no fixed color or shape of its own. It's clear, transparent, and refreshing. Then thought comes in and colors this clear energy with its labels, judgments, and stories. Each thought is like a drop of pigment that releases its color when mixed into water. So when the pure energy of this genuine mind is mixed with thought, what do you get? Our mind becomes very colorful, bright, and expressive—and this is what we call "emotions."

In the end, what's in this potent emotional drink (not like those purple and pink vitamin drinks with no vitamins)? There are only two components: energy and concept. Energy that is bright, refreshing, nourishing, and sustaining, and the dualistic thoughts that color and even flavor that energy. That's all. Put them together and you have a truly energizing drink!

Now that energy and concept are together, conceptual mind starts linking things that are unrelated, and we just go along with that. "Don't wash my lucky shirt! There's a big game today." "How did that guy from Jersey get a better grade than me—he must have cheated!" And that's how we start making things up.

Our conceptual mind is very smart about giving this energy a color and a flavor. And just as smart about giving it a location. Because, in reality, the energy of our emotions has no location. It's clear, open, spacious, and bright, a field of energy that has no boundary. It precedes every concept and predates any reference point. In it, there is no such thing as "me," "you," "here," or "there." So the job of our conceptual mind is to nail it down to a single spot. To make it into something we can relate to with our thoughts. So it assigns this open energy a location and a sense of relationship.

Without that, we are totally lost in this world. Location and relationship are the key points to our feeling that everything's all right and our world makes sense. That's why Google is so important. If you don't know where you are, bring out your phone. Open Google Maps to "my current location." It will tell you where you are, and what direction to go. So this is what our conceptual mind is doing all the time. It's developing a sense of a tangible reality that includes a place for us to be and for others to be. This allows us to relate back and forth in all kinds of ways. All these things working together make our emotional mind more intensely colorful, vivid, and bright. This quality of emotions is like the fizz in soda pop. It perks up what would otherwise be a pretty boring, flat drink.

There's no doubt that emotions are the driving force in our life. Anger, jealousy, passion, fear. At the same time, when we really look at our emotions it's very difficult to find any solid entity called "anger" or "passion." Outside of these two, energy and concept, there's nothing else. There's nothing substantial or solid, nothing we can get hold of.

When we're having a typical bout of anger (energy plus concept) that's an expression of the energy's disturbing, conflicted quality. When these two come together, the expression could go either way. We could experience it as rough or smooth, negative or positive. But if you look purely at the energy level of the anger, you discover that its actual nature is compassion. There's a basic sense of gentleness, warmth, and openness in this energy field, and also an experience of a powerful creative potential.

One time I was watching the video of a teaching given by one of our older lineage masters. He was teaching on the *Heart Sutra*, the Buddha's classic teaching on emptiness. The sutra describes quite beautifully how everything is empty, without essence. And then this master began saying how bad the emotions are, how negative, and that we absolutely must overcome them and realize their empty nature. Then a Western student in the audience asked, "Well, then, if we have to let go of all emotions, how can we be creative?" That's a reasonable question.

Most modern cultures understand that emotions contribute to our creativity. We have so many beautiful songs inspired by these difficult emotions. Just listen to the blues, country music, and rock and roll! It's all there—the disappointment and regret, longing, jealousy, blame, all the hopes and fears that come from our passion.

One of my students loves classical music. She was helping me for a while by driving me around to appointments and on errands. She was constantly listening to Beethoven, Schubert, and all those guys. So I had no choice but to listen to them, too (instead of my usual Guns N' Roses). But I discovered that this classical music is powerfully affective, so pure and direct, simply a different approach to the same heart of compassion.

So emotions are definitely a source of creativity. But the real source of creativity is this pure energy that has no concept, thought, or label attached to it. It's a moment of pure awareness and energy instead of concept and energy. You may have some labeling thoughts just before or just after, but in that moment there is no label. It's what any genuine artist might tell you—when the painter paints, there are moments when the brush just flows. It's the same for poets, sculptors, and of course musicians. There's this sense of "muse" or embodiment of inspiration, which actually lives within all of us. When we're visited by this muse, there's a sense of creative power operating without our conscious effort.

Sometimes this experience can be provoked by strong emotions. Like strong passion or strong aggression. But we have to be careful if we enter that territory. We need to be sure we can work with the energy. Remember, there are two components that will be right there. Concept will be dancing with the energy, too. If you can't tell them apart, you may end up going toward the concept, where the creativity is stifled. Then you'll just feel frustrated. But if you learn how to connect with the energy and can let it be without trying to shape it to your thoughts, it's a beautiful, illuminating experience. What happens in these moments is up to each individual.

Anyway, to continue the story. When I was watching this video, the master was saying, "Oh, no, all emotions are bad. They must be let go. They must be transmuted." So you can see that there's some kind of East-West culture gap in our understanding of emotions. However, from the basic teachings of the Buddha, there is no such gap. Culturally we can have many different views, opinions, and experiences, and that's what we call interpretation. There are different interpretations of the Buddha's teachings. This book represents my own interpretation, based on both traditional Vajrayana Buddhist teachings like *The Aspiration of Samantab-*

hadra* from the Nyingma or Dzogchen lineage, and many teachings from the Mahamudra tradition. These are my main sources for the view of emotions presented here. So from the Vajrayana Buddhist point of view, this bright, clear, creative energy is what emotions are.

---

* See *Penetrating Wisdom: The Aspiration of Samantabhadra,* by Dzogchen Ponlop Rinpoche (Snow Lion Publications, 2006).

16

Restoring Balance

*Fame changes a lot of things,
but it can't change a lightbulb.*

—GILDA RADNER

IF WE CAN be straightforward and honest about who we are
in our day-to-day life, that's an excellent beginning for developing trust in ourselves—the kind of trust that gives us
the confidence to go where we want to go and achieve what
we want to achieve.

When we start out in life, it's our job to learn how to
present ourselves to the world in order to become successful
or just to survive. Our social life and livelihood depend on
our public image. But we've been at it so long that at some
point we forget which part of this public display is "me" and
which is the part we worked so hard to create. This isn't
exactly a new situation. In a way, it's our human condition,
heightened by the times and the state of our culture. The
problem is that we often end up overfeeding our sense of

self-importance until we're lost inside a bloated ego with an inflated sense of pride.

But we don't have to put ourselves down or beat ourselves up! The point is not to self-deprecate but to be more realistic in seeing who we are and to develop some sense of respect, appreciation, and joy in our situation. And relating to others with the same sense of respect and appreciation. We can have a sense of humor about it, too. This bloated, overexaggerated self is like the Bart Simpson balloon I saw in the Macy's Thanksgiving Day parade. Five stories high! The "real" Bart Simpson (if we can say that) is a small boy.

When we look at others, we're doing the same thing—inflating their qualities, but primarily their negative ones. We cherish ourselves and our "superior" qualities and take a little pleasure in seeing the inferior qualities of others. It's a lopsided affair that works in favor of our disturbing emotions. They come out of it the big winners.

According to the Buddhist teachings, what we need to do to bring our relationships into balance (to the relief of everyone) is to take a humble position, lower than the one we think we possess. We have to come down to earth. In Tibetan, we have a saying, something like, "The higher you go, the harder you fall." I think there's a similar saying in English.

What this implies is that when we make it to the top, we're very happy about it. But the air is thin up there and there's not much ground beneath us. Our celebrities and politicians show us all the time that the more famous and powerful you become, the more unstable your position is. You may have been well liked and popular on your way up, but those same fans and supporters may take a different view of you once you're in the top tier of Hollywood or Wall Street or DC. They may start to criticize you and try to take you down. If you're naturally low to the ground, you're not in a precarious position. The winds blow more furiously at the top.

This adjustment in the balance of influence is a mind-training practice. It's training to reduce your inflated ego and pride. Genuine humility is not about denying your good qualities and literally dropping to your knees before the other people in your life. You don't have to become insignificant to be humble. In a sense, mind-training is a trick. It works something like boot camp in the military, where the drill sergeant skillfully breaks down whatever pride you had before you joined the Army. That's similar to the training of new monks in monasteries, by the way. While we're getting rid of our inflated pride and false perception of self by placing ourselves in a humble position, we try to look at others with new eyes and see their positive qualities, viewing them as greater than our own. Not only that, we go a little further and make an effort to actually care for others. We try to feel for another human being the kind of cherishing we've kept almost exclusively for ourselves. Our children may be the exception.

While this may seem dubious at first, the Buddhist teachings say that if you're able to take a humble position—

remaining modest and unpretentious—all good qualities will naturally expand and flourish. And it's taught that the reverse is equally true. If you increase your self-cherishing and pride, then it's very difficult for good qualities to develop at all.

This is a helpful practice because we sometimes don't notice the good qualities of others. We miss what they have to offer. We could be working next to someone who spends their weekends tutoring children and cleaning up their neighborhood. Or who has just written a novel that will become an Oscar-nominated movie. But we never see past the physical space they take up. We see them every day and are annoyed by the same thought: *How did Howard get the good office?*

Some people are naturally "hidden" types, intentionally (on their part) overlooked, never displaying their qualities for others to see. There are many such stories in the Buddhist tradition of enlightened yogis being dismissed as useless beggars or fools until circumstances unfolded to reveal their extraordinary qualities of wisdom and compassion. Then how shocked and embarrassed their critics were!

In the beginning, this type of humility doesn't come naturally. We're so accustomed to thinking we're right. We know which TV shows to watch, the right side of the low-carb versus low-fat debate, what's wrong with the economy, who should and shouldn't be president. And we know all this a little bit better than our spouse or neighbor or the person sitting next to us at our friend's dinner party. That's how we hold ourselves as supreme, as a shade above whoever may have a different opinion. It feels so normal, we don't even realize we're doing it.

It's like we're each the CEO of our world, whatever world that is. We've forgotten that we ever had to look for a job or work in the mailroom. Or maybe it's like starring in our own reality TV show. We're at the center of all the dramas, and while others disappear from the action, there's always a place for us. But now we're trading places, elevating everyone we've walked past without noticing or caring to notice. We're offering our own chair, the comfortable seat by the window, to our teammates and rivals alike.

This takes some getting used to. "Getting used to" means trying many times. But it must be genuine. If you can really do it for even one moment, that's enough. You don't have to worry about holding the thought of cherishing others for a whole week or month. It's impossible to hold the same thought continuously anyway. Something else always pops into your mind. In your history lecture, maybe it's your math homework. At work on a rainy day, maybe it's a dream of blue skies, sandy beaches, and palm trees. All you need to do is keep trying, because even a single moment of sincere regard for another being is precious. Just keep collecting those moments.

You'll notice that when you do this training of restoring balance or "taking a humble position," you're inviting your emotions to rise up and object. So you'll need to look out for them. Desire, attachment, aggression, pride, jealousy, and no doubt ignorance will take this opportunity to try to throw you off your game. What you need to do, as soon as you catch one of them sneaking up on you, is to hit it right on the head. You need to burst its bubble before it bursts yours.

Sometimes we miss the first flicker of our emotions because of a lack of mindfulness, or we may just be feeling lazy in that moment. We don't want to work so hard all the time. What harm is there in a tiny spark of irritation? But while you're drinking your coffee, it becomes a small flame, and by the time you start to worry, you're looking at a forest fire. All the residents in the area are packing up and running for their lives.

Once your disturbing emotions blow up, your usual antidotes don't work. Your fire extinguisher and garden hose are useless. Even the water-bombing helicopters turn back at some point. That little irritation that morphs so quickly into rage will eventually play itself out. It will exhaust itself and curl back up into innocent sleep. But how long until it wakes up again, rested, restored, and ready to go?

Negative emotional patterns that have a strong foothold in our lives are less responsive to any sort of antidote, spiritual or mundane. The mindfulness practices and traditional therapies will both have a tougher time cutting through this kind of deeply rooted confusion. So the instructions say don't ignore any negative habitual patterns when you see them. No matter how pretty and harmless a small spark seems to be, as soon as it arises, smash it down with mindfulness and compassion.

Once you've applied the antidote, let it go. The moment is gone. Don't hold on to it. This is important to remember because sometimes after the disturbing emotion is over, we get stuck in the antidote. We keep applying it uselessly. So once the emotion's vanished there's no need to ask, *Where has it gone?* Just let go and relax.

When we talk about inflated ego and pride as obstacles and suggest practices to put ourselves in a "lower" position, this can be a challenge if we are struggling with personal issues like feelings of inferiority or low self-esteem. When you're trying to build yourself up to a healthy norm, these mind-training practices may feel like you're going backward. I have appreciated hearing this perspective from Buddhist practitioners, new and old, who speak from firsthand experience. Again, there are cultural differences at play. As Buddhism travels from culture to culture, there are differences in psychologies and customs that need to be identified and respected.

So to be clear, the point of this exercise in humility is to get in touch with the reality of who you are. It's not about putting yourself down. On this path, there is no intention to disparage or undermine anyone, ever. We are trying to see clearly how we create this persona, this ego-self called by a certain name and known by certain attributes, and how it all becomes so inflated or distant from our most genuine self. It's a process intended to help us see that and come back to the reality of who, what, and where we are. On the other hand, being humble here simply means having a genuine respect for other human beings. It means we can live in this world with the same sense of appreciation and regard for others as we hold for ourselves.

In all cases, respect your own experience and adopt what works for you. There are so many methods, there's no need to stick with something that's not helping you. Whatever you're doing, don't push too hard. If one method turns out to be an emotional trigger for you, it's better to let it go. You can always try again later after learning more about it. Or you can simply enjoy the experience of cherishing others. Just focus on that alone and the benefit will naturally be the same as restoring balance by taking a lower seat. Either way, your whole world is elevated.

℈ CONTEMPLATION ON THE EQUALITY OF SELF AND OTHER

This contemplation supports the training in "restoring balance" or "equalizing self and other." It's described here as a group exercise, but it can also be done individually. If you're working with this exercise alone, then whenever the instructions say to "look at the person" to your left or right, simply think of someone you know, and take them as your focus.

To Begin (Five Minutes)

Seated in a comfortable, relaxed, and upright posture, bring your attention lightly to the movements of the breath and allow your mind and body to gradually settle. When thoughts arise, simply let them go and return to the present moment.

The Practice

Once you feel settled and present, bring to mind the person on your right. Think how that person, although separate from you and unknown in many ways, shares many life experiences. Everyone wakes up each day wishing for happiness, wishing for fortunate circumstances to support them and their families. Yet we all experience loss, pain, and disappointment. We are all subject to the same hopes and fears. What sufferings has the person on your right faced in their life? What losses overshadow their joys? What's yet to come for them?

Now think how wonderful it would be if that person could be truly happy, if they could be free of all suffering and fear. Then make an aspiration or wish for that person in your own words, such as, *May this person be completely free of all suffering right now, in this moment. Instead of pain and struggle, may their life be full of happiness.* Contemplate for a few minutes how happy you would feel if your wish for them was fulfilled. Now think, *The happiness of this person is more important to me in this moment than my own. My own happiness is only increased by their happiness.*

Now turn your attention to the person on your left and contemplate in the same way on their sufferings and happiness. (*In a group setting, you can continue and think of the person in front of you and behind you, etc.*)

Next, bring to mind anyone you know (*anywhere in the world*) who is suffering and think how wonderful it would be if they could be free of all their grief and pain. Now make an aspiration for them, wishing that all their suffering might be liberated, gone in this very moment, and replaced with peace and happiness.

You can contemplate cherishing anyone, whether you know them or not. You can think of anyone who suffers in any way—from physical or mental illness, chronic pain, poverty, violence, or unhappiness of any kind. You can also bring to mind those who are dying or have passed away and those left behind. You can change your focus from those you know to those you learn about and see on TV and other news media. This is how we practice equalizing self and other.

To Close (Five Minutes)

Conclude with a few minutes of simple sitting meditation. You can also take a moment to appreciate how everyone in your group for this brief time was wishing for the happiness of those around them. You can make your own aspiration to extend your caring for others a little more each day.

17

Dealing with Difficult People

If you don't like something, change it.
If you can't change it, change your attitude.

—MAYA ANGELOU

WHEN WE'RE READY to test our progress in reversing our negative emotions, there's nothing like working with difficult people. Can we extend our kindness beyond our usual limits? Can we break through our fears? We might be thinking, *Damn the torpedoes, full speed ahead!* until we come face-to-face with the first person who could help us answer these questions. Hopefully, that's a moment when we can use all our emergency training, and then see what happens when we reach out and make a connection.

How great it would be if we could just lend a hand to all the nice people out there, the ones who are easy to deal with, always pleasant and gracious. But they're the ones who always seem to have people lining up to help them out. So there's no need for us to join that crowd. The people who need our help are the ones who don't have anybody to call:

the kind of people nobody wants to go near, the difficult-to-bear, the ones who cause lots of problems. What you can do for these people, at least, is give rise to compassion instead of animosity. And if you feel you can go further, if you really want to try to reach out to someone and be helpful, these are the ones who need it the most.

If you limit your compassionate activities to people who are easy, attractive, and full of fun, then whatever you do, whatever actions you perform, may not necessarily be genuine compassion. There's a kind of self-serving aspect to what you do. How much of your commitment is tied to having a good time? We touch the real heart of compassion when we can engage with someone who is suffering from carrying so much aggression, so much negativity, so much emotion that they can't help but cause trouble and drive people away. If you can approach such a person and give them some support, then maybe there is some actual compassion there. This is one of the Buddha's teachings on the courageous and noble heart of compassion. It's challenging, but you can try it and see what happens. The good thing for us is that this teaching doesn't say we have to stay with that person forever. The point is to grow our heart of kindness and love for all. That includes difficult people. It doesn't say that we have to be around them all the time.

In the beginning, it's impossible for most of us to transform our disturbing emotions immediately, simply with mindfulness. We notice we're full of angry feelings and thoughts and we tell ourselves, *I believe in being positive, so just get over it!* Doubtful. So another approach is to "transform through conduct" first. "Conduct" means "actions," and here we are talking about what we do with our body and speech, which are expressions of our emotions and intentions. We need to observe and work with both. Working with our conduct is a more manageable approach because it's immediate and concrete. You don't have to guess, *Did I just push Sam out of the way? Or was that a bear hug?* You know.

Awareness of our actions is also key to seeing how we can befriend and support difficult people, including those who are only difficult for us. That can happen, too. We meet a friend of a friend and intuitively feel mistrust or caution instead of interest and openness. But whatever our habits are, they're sure to show up in force when we're in an intensified situation. Working with an awareness of our body language and speech can help us get a grip on our thoughts and emotions, which are the mental equivalent of walking and talking.

WORKING FROM THE OUTSIDE IN

If you have a strong habit of reacting with anger when criticized, for example, it will take only a little mindfulness to see when you're acting that out in an obvious way. You start by directing your attention toward yourself, not toward your critic. Look at your own actions, your own conduct, rather than the actions or words of anyone else. You don't even need to think about the emotion itself at this point. You only need to be clear about your own actions in the present moment.

If you feel you're about to get into a confrontation with someone, or just another hurtful conversation, stop for a moment (breathe). Now look at your conduct. What are you doing with your body? Where is it? How is it? Are you leaning into or away from that person? What are your hands doing? Where are your eyes looking? Physical gestures are powerful communicators of feelings and intentions. So, be aware. Tell yourself to drop any behavior that signals hostility or threat. Stop pointing fingers or clenching your fists. Relax your gaze, sit or stand straight. These are things you can control once you notice them. You can even add a smile.

In the same way, look at your speech. Are you using harsh language? How loudly are you talking? How fast or slow? Again, be aware of any verbal signals you're sending (groaning, giggling) in addition to your actual words. Tell yourself to drop any verbal expressions that incite you or the person you're talking to. Consciously lowering your voice and avoiding inflammatory speech are things you can choose to do once you bring a sense of mindfulness to your actions.

At this point, we're working from the outside in. Every positive external change we make helps to calm our inner disturbances. It may help to remember this: when you're so angry or jealous that your hands are shaking, your body is twisted, and your voice has dropped to a whisper or risen to a shriek, it's not only obvious to you—everybody notices.

Before You Go

When you know you're going to be working with a difficult person, before jumping in too deeply you can prepare by bringing to mind the misery of such a negative existence and imagining how painful that must be. When you begin to feel a sense of sympathy and openness, you can take the next step. You can move a little closer. Spend some time together and see what happens—see if there is any possibility of a positive interaction. If things are looking up for a while, but then take a turn for the worse, it's best to retreat. If you find yourself losing patience or sympathy, and you can see the benefit of your efforts flying out the window, simply step back for a while. It's better than getting caught up in a conflicted situation that will produce more harm. You can always try again later.

The pain of making this kind of effort isn't really as bad as we imagine. It's like going to the dentist. Sitting in that chair with light shining in your eyes and sharp objects poking into every corner of your mouth isn't pleasant, but the anticipation is worse. At least for me. Thinking about it the week before is more agonizing than actually being there. I'm always tempted to cancel. But if I can just get myself there, it's not that bad. And dentists are usually such nice people.

When we think about difficult people, we're usually thinking of someone else, but we ourselves might fall into that category, too, at least occasionally. So whatever recommendations we have for working with "those people" applies to us as well. We all have our moments. We've all been called "difficult" (or worse) by someone at some time. We're probably lucky we don't know who said it, and how many times.

FIERCE SUFFERING

Another group of difficult people are those afflicted with "fierce suffering." These are people who are difficult for us for different reasons. Their suffering may be so great, the difficulty lies in facing it. Often and tragically they're innocent of fault. There are many examples all over the world—debilitating physical and mental illnesses, loss and injury due to abuse, exploitation, violence, war, poverty, and natural disasters.

If we have an opportunity to help one person with such fierce suffering, that is a great benefit. If we can do more, that's wonderful. If we cannot help directly, we may be able to help indirectly by supporting those on the ground offering food, medicine, and consolation. Doctors Without Borders and similar organizations go wherever there is great suffering, great need, and few resources. They are our modern-day saints or bodhisattvas. If we cannot go to these places ourselves, we can offer monetary gifts and also use social media to bring attention to their work in areas of critical need, actions that will inspire others to help as well. There are many ways we can help directly or indirectly; we just have to find the opportunities that make sense for our lives. When we do engage in compassionate activities, we should not judge. Leave all that behind. Just help.

THE VERY, VERY BAD

It's hard enough to work with our own emotions, and "difficult" people offer an even greater challenge. But what do we do when it comes to people whose actions are inconceivable to us? How are we supposed to regard people who intentionally inflict great harm on others—the murderers, child abusers, and terrorists? We want them to be punished, to understand and feel the pain they have rained down on others. We want society to be safe and we want justice.

How does all this talk about compassion relate to this situation? Is it an exception? Are we expected to treat people who are responsible for committing real atrocities the same way we treat those we care about and love, who are really good people? How can we, or should we?

We can look at this situation in different ways. On an ordinary, relative level, we can see such people as totally ignorant. For whatever reason, their natural awareness is deluded. Their minds are dark, blinded by ignorance. Sadly, they're cut off from their inherent wisdom and compassion. People like this often don't realize the magnitude of pain and suffering they've caused in the world. Although they understand right from wrong in the legal sense, we can at least say that spiritually, or humanly, they are totally deaf and dumb to the suffering they plan and execute.

To be that person is unthinkable to us. They're not only guilty, they're universally condemned and reviled, and so we can feel a spark of compassion for them. We can even go further and feel what they cannot feel—unbiased compassion for their tragic state. This is not an automatic response we can just bring to mind and then say, "Yes, I love you and forgive you." It is genuinely difficult and even frightening to approach such darkness. Yet such a person needs love from somewhere, if there is any hope for them at all. Those who are able can pray for them.

From a more ultimate point of view, we can remember that the nature of mind of all sentient beings is fundamentally pure and awake. Even the worst, most deluded person has some positive qualities, some spark of wakefulness and goodness. We may not see that spark because of the prevailing darkness, but we have to be fair and allow that much. We have to say, okay, maybe there is some chance.

When we hear outcries for justice, it's questionable whether standard punishments can achieve that. What we really want is the crime undone, life restored. We can't do that or take away the pain. But perhaps we could go beyond the traditional notion of punishment—of locking people up behind iron bars with nothing meaningful to do. I think we do hold the idea of "justice" as a force for good, but we're also stuck with "punishment." If we combined them a little differently, with the intention of understanding and respecting the needs of all sides, we might achieve a greater degree of balance in the system. We could say that real punishment for a person of this type would be putting them in an environment that cultivated qualities of love and kindness and gave them ways to practice it. They would probably naturally gravitate toward a more aggressive and negative environment if given a choice. They might enjoy the fighting and confusion.

So the real "correction facility" would be a means of transforming behavior through education and time spent in positive activities in a healthy environment. If this would help such callous and desensitized people to wake up and recognize the suffering and harm they caused, and to feel genuine regret, perhaps that is real justice, a return to goodness, and something to hope for.

PATIENCE

There are many kinds of patience, and misunderstandings of it as well. It's considered a virtue, but also kind of a boring way to be good. As we said earlier, practicing patience doesn't mean you're simply being passive, bravely (or "virtuously") assuming a "waiting-it-out" attitude. When you're dealing with the emotions, the essence of patience is staying with whatever you're feeling without reacting to it. You do this again and again, each time the emotion returns and you have the urge to immediately react. When we're in the position of dealing with difficult people or those who offer particular challenges to us, patience can teach us a lot and practicing it can virtually transform our experience.

The first kind of patience we learn to practice in this situation is "making light of" the harm or negativity directed at us by someone we're trying to relate to. Maybe your boss asks you to work with John to get a project completed on time. You know that no one else wants to do it. They all happen to be very busy. John is smart, articulate, talented, and also a total control freak, suspicious and jealous of anyone who has a dissenting opinion. You decide you're going to be positive. You're going to follow John's lead and not get caught in any messy misunderstandings. Hahaha. That is so unlikely because your rational thought doesn't speak the language of John's emotions. Now is the time you need to practice this kind of "making light of" patience not only to get you through the experience, but also to break the nearly inevitable pattern of suffering and pain. You can help yourself and John, too.

So when John starts to criticize or belittle your work (as expected), the wise response is patience, holding still, allowing space. Whether John has found a legitimate error or is dreaming the whole thing up, you know that his intention is probably to hurt you personally and disparage you professionally. So to be patient isn't easy. But whether or not you're innocent of all fault, you don't let yourself respond right away. You don't fight back by criticizing him or trying to take him down in the same way. You don't even need to deny or correct his accusations. The main point is that when blame comes your way, when the words of a friend or enemy or stranger slap you in the face, the first thing to do is practice patience. Hold still for a moment. One moment. That moment can change the outcome. It allows space for something else to happen.

As we know in our daily life, we usually don't respond well when we're criticized or accused of something, especially unfairly. We might start defending ourselves before the other person has finished going over their list of complaints. I had a funny experience recently driving in Seattle. I was stopped at a traffic light. It was a chilly day and my windows were rolled up. But I noticed the couple in the car next to me. I couldn't hear anything but they were quite animated, and it looked like they might be having fun, singing to some loud music. At the next traffic light they were still singing. So I rolled down my window, and instead of music, heard that they were actually shouting at each other. Both screaming at the same time. I was so surprised, I thought, *What's the point? Who's listening? Nobody.* They were alone in the car. They didn't seem too interested in what the other one might be saying. Then the light changed, and we went our own ways.

When we're talking over another person, drowning them out, responding instantly, or even talking too fast, then nobody hears anything. There is no space; there is no gap in between. The point of speaking to each other is usually to communicate. We talk and listen to clarify what we mean, say what we feel, and generally understand each other. We don't do it to become more confused or because we enjoy hurt feelings. We are hoping for a positive outcome. In reality, though, sometimes talking makes things worse. So a good lesson to learn is that we don't need to say anything right away, especially in significant or sensitive situations. I think your lawyer would give you the same advice! Take your time, take a few breaths, and relax.

REDUCING DEFENSIVENESS

When someone is criticizing us (deserved or not) and pointing out our faults, we want to come back with some counterargument. It's "Yes, but . . . !" or "No, you don't understand . . . !" Even when we realize we have made some mistake, we want to defend ourselves.

Along with developing patience, we need to reduce our defensiveness. As we increase one quality that will help us, we decrease one that never does. As long as we hang on to our defensive attitude, we'll have problems getting in tune with others or living harmoniously wherever we perceive difference.

That defensive mind is a state of delusion because it blocks our "pure vision." In defense mode, our mental state is less clear, less precise, and we're less likely to see the positive qualities of others. At the same time, our intention to benefit others is blocked. Not exactly the outcome we want.

So we continue our training in mindfulness. We think of others, including difficult people, and act with compassion. And we try to be patient even as we become a target of harsh words and blame. Gradually our defensiveness loosens up and finally dissolves. We loosen up, too, and lighten up.

It's best to start this practice with something small. That's fine for a while. Don't leap into anything big, like a divorce settlement or a dispute with the IRS. You can continue to rely on your lawyer for these things! A small thing is like your sweet but troubled roommate insisting that your copy of *The Invisible Man* (which you left last night on the kitchen table) is hers. *She remembers lending it to you.* You know she lent her copy to someone else, but you've already read it and you got it used, so . . . she can have it. You don't say anything. Or someone bumps into you and turns to you and says, "Watch where you're going . . . [expletive]!" That's okay. That guy is the one whose day just got a little worse.

Again, this is mind-training. You learn from it and then move on with the wisdom you've gained. As you keep at it, you become more at ease in all your relationships.

℘ MORE PATIENT, LESS DEFENSIVE

(Two-person speaking and listening exercises.)

These exercises are intended to help you increase your ability to tolerate intense emotional situations while maintaining mindfulness and a sense of empathy. As in the previous "speaking and listening" exercises, you work with a partner, exchanging roles midway. It's helpful to affirm in the beginning that the intention of both parties is to benefit and support the other. It is also fine to pause or stop the exercise at any time if either of you becomes uncomfortable.

To begin, sit quietly facing your partner (*two minutes*).

Each of you will have an opportunity to act as the listener as well as the speaker, for a period of two minutes. Then you'll be able to share your experience for five minutes after each.

The Speaker

The speaker's job is to direct several negative, judgmental, blaming remarks to the listener. The intention is not to actually criticize or correct the listener's character or behavior, but to give him/her an opportunity to experience mindfully what it feels like to be judged, especially unfairly. Be direct (avoiding yelling or excessive criticism), but it's all right to say something like, "You are bad at this . . . You are always doing . . ." This is an opportunity for you to mindfully experience what it feels like to speak unkindly or harshly to someone who is right in front of you.

❖ For one minute, direct a series of critical, judgmental, or blaming remarks to your partner. Stay visually connected to him/her.

❖ Notice what emotions are coming up for you as you're speaking. How does it feel to say these things? At the same time, look at your partner. Can you sense how your remarks are affecting him/her?

❖ For the next minute, keep your seat as the speaker but remain silent. Notice how you're feeling physically and what emotions you're feeling in the aftermath.

The Listener

❖ While listening to the list of your imperfections and defects, simply try to remain present in your

body and mindful of the emotions that come up
for you. Keeping a visual awareness of the speaker
may help you stay present.

❖ Watch your mind while the speaker is talking to
you, but don't react, don't fight back, and don't
deny or attempt to correct any of the accusations.

❖ In the following moment of silence, notice how
you feel—see what emotions come up for you.

Speaker and Listener

❖ Take five minutes after completing the exercise to
share your experiences. Encourage each other to
share, ask questions, and end on a positive note.

❖ Sit quietly together for another minute or two.

Speaker and listener switch roles and repeat the exercise.

Variations

Repeat the exercise, with these changes:

❖ In this variation, after the speaker's negative
comments, the listener responds with a positive
observation about the speaker, followed by a
moment of mindful silence.

❖ In this variation, the comments made by the speaker are all positive, constructive remarks about the listener's good qualities.

❖ If you do not have a partner to work with, you can do these exercises alone in front of a mirror. In this case, you are simultaneously the speaker and listener, noticing all the emotions triggered for you as the words are spoken and received. Instead of sharing your experiences with a partner, you can write in your journal for five or ten minutes afterward.

18

A Vision of Peace

There can never be peace between nations
until there is first known that true peace
which is within the souls of men.

—BLACK ELK

THESE DAYS IT seems that most Western Buddhists are liberals, both politically and socially. At the same time, there are certainly many places in the world where Buddhists hold traditional and conservative views. However, most are progressive, which we can attribute to the Buddha. Thousands of years ago, the Buddha broke with many cultural values and practiced forms of equal rights that were unheard of in his time. The tradition of the Buddha with his emphasis on nonviolence, equality, and tolerance is continued today by Buddhist teachers.

Like many people today, Buddhists share a vision of a peaceful world, free of war and aggression. But even if we are waving NO NUKES banners (and the like) on the streets, or metaphorically in our lectures, blogs, and tweets, we haven't fully disarmed ourselves. We haven't set aside our own aggression.

Too often, we do the opposite of what we say. In the microcosm of our own world, we wage our private wars on one another. How often do we respond to someone's anger at us with anger, impatience, and defensiveness? When our spouse blames us for one thing, we try to find some other blame to pin on him or her. And on it goes, as if none of this counted as war or aggression or a fundamental disturbance of the peace.

Our basic principles of peace and harmony and nonviolence can all go down the drain when it comes to our own individual ways of relating with each other. If we act in this way, our noble view and our actual practice have become two separate things. We can have a high view, but our practice doesn't usually line up with that view.

When it comes to the views of political parties, the liberals accuse the conservatives and the conservatives accuse the liberals of wrong views and flip-flopping back and forth. It's easy to claim you hold the high moral ground, but it's our actions that reveal what is in our hearts and minds. When the rhetoric of animosity, harsh language, and blame are praised far and wide, and the intention behind this rhetoric is clearly to harm, then there is no moral ground to stand on. There is no vision to uplift, to benefit, or to protect anyone.

In whatever way we can, it's important for us to think about peace, what it really means to us. Can we see ourselves establishing our vision of a perfect foreign policy in our domestic relationships? Can we bring our most idealistic vision of world peace into our very own lives?

Since many of us don't rule the world, how do we change it? Each one of us changes it by practicing peace, practicing patience, and practicing loving-kindness and compassion at home. Where the heart is.

DOWNTOWN "YOGI"

In the solitude
Of the skyscrapers' jungle
I find neon lights
Shine like watermoons

Traffic flows
Like a beautiful river
And TV's echo
Like the sound of thoughts in a cave

Mind's still the same
As it was centuries ago
Always with a choice
Of fumbling great opportunities
Or appreciating the beauty of this moment

So I choose to be right here—now
Within all experiences
Without solidifying or rejecting
It's just a story told by this drifter's thought

dpr | 10/07/08 |

"Open Dream" by Dzogchen Ponlop Rinpoche

Index